CONTENTS

Stanley Spencer Remembered

an anthology compiled, edited and updated
by Joan George

Taderon Press
London

Published by Taderon Press, 42 Blythe Rd., London, W14 0HA

ISBN 978-1903656-91-4

Distributed worldwide by
Garod Books Ltd.
42 Blythe Rd.
London, W14 0HA
ENGLAND
Email: *info@garodbooks.com*

This book is dedicated to the memory of

Sir Stanley Spencer, CBE., RA. (1891-1959)

Stanley enjoying a joke with his brother Gilbert

Preface

In the fifty years that have elapsed since Stanley Spencer's untimely death in 1959, much has been written about him and his work. Yet his character had many sides, and this anthology of my own memories and those of his daughters, friends and neighbours, aims to supplement more learned works by showing the humorous, adaptable and (dare I say?) lovable side of the artist.

The idea of a commemoration originated in November 2008, when I noticed an inaccuracy in the local paper, which claimed that it had been more than a hundred years since Stanley Spencer lived at Fernlea. In fact, the house built by his grandfather, had been purchased by concerned patrons in 1958 and placed in trust for the artist and his family. Stanley and Gilbert both spelt the name of the house "Fernley". Other sources use what I assume is the correct spelling, "Fernlea", which I have adopted throughout to avoid the confusion.

I visited the artist at Fernlea in 1958, and 1959 during his last illness. That was not a hundred years ago, but it was a half century back, and therefore due for some sort of commemoration – a reminder that appealed to his many friends and admirers. Their contributions have been an essential part of this anthology, which I have ended in the form of a "letter to Stanley" highlighting the many Spencer-orientated events that have taken place in the last fifty years.

As compiler and editor, I feel that another dimension has been added with the contributions and insights of Stanley's daughters, Shirin and Unity Spencer.

The realisation of the fifty years commemoration came at an inconvenient time for me as an octogenarian. I was looking forward to a break from the literary demands of my lap-top, until I realised that my survival qualified me to recall personal memories of Stanley. We had been good friends for the last four years of his life; I had unpublished material about him and a substantial personal archive of Spencer cuttings. I had to do something about it.

This was difficulat at a time of global economic depression. What about publication, distribution, would it sell? rather like Stanley with his uncommissioned works, I had the vision and carried on.

It meant arranging interviews, editing people's "memories" and doing extensive research once the idea of updating it in the form of a "letter to Stanley" had taken root.

Appropriately, this year's Cookham Festival of the Arts included a light operatic work by a local enthusiast titled: *Another Cookham Resurrection.*

****

Prologue

Looking back to the nature and nurture that combined to form the creative genius of Stanley Spencer, few facts are available apart from the childhood reminiscences of *Stanley Spencer by his Brother Gilbert*. The author described his book as "a kind of backcloth to Stan's life". A cousin gives an alternative view.

Stanley himself asserted that he took from "Pa" his "sense of wonder", and from "Ma" his "small frame and sense of the dramatic". (1) William Spencer's sense of wonder found expression in music (he was a distinguished organist, choir master and piano teacher), and intellectual activity. Stanley's paternal grandfather, Julius a master builder, forged the first links with the local aristocracy. He formed and conducted a village choir, which, according to Gilbert Spencer, "retained some of the traditions of the itinerant musicians; it would be summoned ... often to sing at important houses in the district". On one occasion, "they were invited to sing at Cliveden House, the seat of the Duke of Westminster". (2) The link with Cliveden continued for the next two generations although the patron changed.

Following William's marriage to Anna Slack in 1873 – they had been childhood friends, the relationship developing through their mutual love of music and membership of Julius Spencer's choir – he was unaccountably transferred from his post as organist at Holy Trinity church, Cookham, to a London church. This may have happened via the patronage network. The promotion involved additional benefits in the form of piano pupils, notes Gilbert, "from influential families". The London sojourn enabled William to educate himself further in the classics and foreign languages, and to meet like-minded intellectuals.

Family commitments and a professed "love of Cookham" brought him home as organist and choir master at Hedsor, a tiny church perched on a hill about two miles from Cookham. Lord Boston of Hedsor House was patron of the church, and later, of the Spencers. William soon acquired music pupils – some "widely scattered", writes Gilbert. "He reached them all on his lady's bicycle, his only means of transport throughout his professional life". (3)

Meantime Stanley and Gilbert – escaping their father's pressure on older siblings to study music – had weekly drawing and painting lessons from a neighbour, Miss Dorothy Bailey. Stanley's skill as a painter of flowers owes much to Dorothy's teaching as this was her speciality. Another early influence was, of course, music. Many of William's pupils came to the family home for piano lessons in the dining-room, and Gilbert remembers his sister Annie, reading to the boys at bedtime, then, "propping up her music on the chest of drawers and practising on her viola". (4)

Stanley's mother, Anna Slack, was born in 1851 at Wooburn, the daughter of Mary (née Barnett) and John Slack. From Victorian times this village (about three miles from Cookham), had been a centre for paper manufacture. Gilbert believed that it was the paper mills that attracted the Barnetts to Wooburn, and that "Grandma Barnett" was Jewish. (5) John Slack, he tells us, came from Ireland. He may have been a cobbler, because after his marriage to Mary Barnett they made their home at Cookham, then a centre of the shoe trade. A Mr Burrows had established a cottage industry in cobbling, and John Slack, Gilbert recalls, was "the overseer and chief cutter" for Burrows shoes. (6)

With the decline of Cookham's shoe industry "Grandma Slack" acquired the management of the village grocery and general store. Her youngest daughter, Anna, "an observant little girl" (7) became adept at impersonating the customers. She went from house to house (according to family legend) entertaining the villagers. After her marriage to William, they lived at Fernlea, (built by Julius Spencer), "for the rest of their lives", Gilbert recalls. (8)

In the late 1960s I met Stanley's cousin, Amy Hagerty Spencer, an unmarried, elderly artist who lived alone in a rambling house full of memories. Ship Orchard and its overgrown garden have now been replaced with a small development of modern houses in Sutton Road between School Lane and the Gallery.

On May 22nd 1967 Amy wrote to "The Managers of the King's Hall Gallery", setting out three columns showing the branches of the Spencer family descending from her "Great-Grandfather Julius". Her father and his family had moved from Cookham to north London in the 1890s, but they returned on many occasions to visit her grandparents at Vine Cottage (almost opposite Fernlea in the High Street).

She remembered seeing Stanley and Gilbert in the garden at Fernlea sitting in their high-chairs. "They were very late learning to walk". In the letter she listed her qualifications: "I hold First Class Government Certificates for all Art Subjects, and am entitled to take an Art School – therefore I know the difference between distorted art (since 1914) and really good work". She quotes a leading Cookham resident who "had the courage to call Stanley's work "ugly", I would go further and say some of it is downright hideous ... " She continued:

"Stanley's memory was quite unreliable, and people who [have] read Gilbert's books said he spoke and told tales about his Grandfather Julius, as though he knew him, whereas he never could have met him".

Amy had forgotten the Spencer gift for storytelling from one generation to the next. In her final salvo, she suggested: "If you should wish for any correct information – I shall be glad to give it – at Ship Orchard.

Yours faithfully,

Amy Hagerty Spencer". (9)

As Hon. Secretary to the Trustees of the Gallery, I was asked to reply to the letter. I referred to Stanley's originality, sincerity and his minute study of detail. A few days later she wrote, telling me of their teenage arguments:

"Cross him and point out his errors, and he would get in a scarlet temper. The reason we argued was because I knew that a proper groundwork was necessary to enable anyone to tackle and carry out any artwork ... His theory that people must not be taught, but go their own way is apparent in his work, where the same errors remain to this day". She summed up by describing Stanley and his family as "perverse" and "cussed ..." (10)

It would be easy to dismiss Amy's criticism as jealousy, or sour grapes, but I remember her as a passionate, proud woman fiercely sincere in her beliefs. It was a sad irony that despite her qualifications and "groundwork" her life's work amounted to little, while Stanley, the rule-breaker, was celebrated and loved.

Thus into Stanley's inherited melting-pot went a touch of the Orient, from the Barnetts, in addition to his broad interest in Eastern religions and culture; John Slack's practical skills, and his mother's gift of mimicry combined with a sense of humour. The family's legacy of patronage descended to Stanley and his siblings. It was Lady Boston of Hedsor House who sent the artist to the Slade School of Art.

It would be fascinating if the modern science of DNA were applied to Stanley. As Adrian Glew, who edited some of his writings, has observed, he was forever analysing his many "selves". He wrote to Hilda that he "would like to compile a family tree of all the selves in spite of their *remoteness* from each other"... (11) Some of these "selves" found expression in his paintings, others in the copious writings and yet more in his indiscreet confidences to friends and acquaintances.

There was much of his father in Stanley's intellectual tastes and ambition, but this was complicated by indecision regarding how best to express these momentous "notions and predilections". His keen observation, and enjoyment of an audience came from his mother, but his many other "selves" clamoured for expression too, and it was perhaps for this reason that he was unable to provide posterity with a coherent explanation of his figurative paintings. His daughters, Shirin and Unity, describe in detail how his work evolved from "Notions and Predilections" to drawings and studies for major pictures. Friends and neighbours glimpse other sides to this amicable genius with large, unfulfilled ideas.

Prologue. Notes and References.

1. Kenneth Pople, *Stanley Spencer,* Collins, London, 1991, p.6.
2. Gilbert Spencer, *Stanley Spencer by his Brother Gilbert,* Victor Gollancz Ltd., 1961, p.16
3. Ibid., p.29.
4. Ibid., p.36.
5. Ibid., p.20.
6. Ibid.
7. Ibid., p.21.
8. Ibid., p.28.
9. Letter in compiler's possession
10. Ibid.
11. Adrian Glew, *Stanley Spencer: Letters and Writings,* Tate Publishing, 2001, p.216

****

"Notions and Predilections"

Some observations by his daughters of Stanley Spencer's ideas behind his drawings and studies.

"First he had these notions", Shirin writes. "He would have a huge idea, like a book, and then the chapters would be different drawings consisting of all these little notions which, once he had done them he didn't change or move them around. He never talked about an idea, or a concept, only about notions and predilections. When he was drawing a notion, it was complete within itself, completely concentrated. It was the marriage between himself and that particular notion, place, or person, and the predilections he connected with that. I think that his own meaning of "predilection" was that he knew before that the thing was both lovable and drawable.

"Then he would organise all these different notions and predilections to form the bigger composition. He had a very strong sense of form, partly visual and partly because he had heard and practised so many fugues – he organised his notions so that they would make a good composition".

"His drawings are works of art", writes Unity, "which lead to a bigger composition. He would have the initial idea, grab the nearest thing to him like an envelope, and do a simple line drawing. After thinking about it and maybe trying it out on a larger scale and squaring it up, with a view to getting it on to canvas. He would do this when he thought that the initial drawing was absolutely right. He wasn't a person to fumble around, occasionally he would make a slight alteration, but the initial impulse was the strong thing.

Unity continued: "When I was a child living at Epsom and he came to stay, I was intrigued to find out how he drew. I used to watch him to see. He always started with the eyes, then he would move out from there. I also noticed he was very careful about sharpening his pencils, he used a knife to get a very fine point.

"I saw him working on the murals he did for Glasgow (*Shipbuilding on the Clyde* series). I would come back from school to see what progress had been made on *Riveters*. I remember being very impressed by the way he drew a straight line. There were taut pieces of rope to draw, and with the canvas flat on the floor, Daddy would lie with his face on the canvas and draw, keeping the pencil as a dot, so that it didn't move from side to side, just kept the same size as a dot. That's how he got a straight line without having to use a ruler.

"I also saw that he never crosshatched: he drew like Leonardo, the Renaissance type of shading which he learned as a student at the Slade – a very fine line full of meaning. He was sensitive about the shading creating the form. The white part of the paper made up the form, the shading was just one aspect of it. When he was drawing it was like meditation – the ego is nowhere around and so you are the sole vehicle".

"For my Father drawing was a voyage towards a very definite destination", writes Shirin, "and there were never any doubts en route. I think his drawings were also like someone doing an experiment. You've got to get all the conditions absolutely right. When he was drawing he looked rather as he did when he was playing the piano, as though he was exploring, creating. He would sort of hold his mouth in a special way as if it were full, and he couldn't hold himself back from feelings welling up inside. When he was drawing from observation there was the same look, but fiercer. The figure of Christ in the Regatta picture has the same expression: exploring and creating at the same time. I remember him saying quietly once that design was the image of the soul".

****

Personal Memories

To clarify the identity of some of the people mentioned in the following Personal Memories, a brief chronology of the first half of Stanley's life may be helpful.

From 1908-1912 he studied at the Slade School of Art, where he was nicknamed "Cookham" because of his attachment to his birthplace and home. Stanley met his first wife, Hilda through his friendship with an artistic London family. In 1919 he wrote:

"Hilda I met at the Carlines' and I was very struck. I thought how extraordinary she looked. I could feel my real self in that extraordinary person. I felt a longing for her, as at once I saw a life with her". Hilda was an artist and an ardent Christian Scientist. They married six years later, when Stanley was working on his famous picture, *Resurrection at Cookham.*

Mr Louis Behrend, a generous patron of the 1920s, built the Sandham Memorial Chapel, near Newbury, for Stanley to decorate with the painted memories of his army service in the First World War. In 1927 when their daughter Shirin was two years old, the family moved into a cottage at Burghclere, near the chapel. At this time Stanley was suffering from renal colic and Hilda had bouts of depression. Life was difficult for them. In 1930 when he had completed the monumental decoration of the chapel, their second daughter Unity was born at Hampstead. Two years later he became an associate member of the Royal Academy, and moved back to Cookham.

The family became friendly with Patricia Preece, an elegant, sophisticated woman living in the village with her artist friend, Dorothy Hepworth. Stanley was mesmerised by Patricia, and had the "notion" of having two wives despite the legal consequences. His friend Richard Kennedy said at the time: "'Stanley is an "innocent"'.

Stanley wrote to Hilda: "Patricia supplies what I miss in you; you supply what I miss in Patricia ..." He had always cherished the idea of marriage, but not to one person alone. He disapproved of mistresses and reluctantly persuaded Hilda to divorce him in 1936. A year later he married Patricia. Heavily in debt due to an excess of expensive present-giving to Patricia, he was no longer attractive to her as a husband, although she had the kudos of being the wife of a famous artist. She continued to live with her partner, Hepworth, and Stanley's dream of two wives left him with none.

It was the memory of Hilda which dominated his thoughts, writings and art until her death in 1950 – and after. He consoled himself by writing almost daily, to his deceased former spouse.

Miss SHIRIN SPENCER recalls: "In the late summer of 1959, I returned from what was then Southern Rhodesia, now Zimbabwe, and went to stay with Stanley at Fernlea. He was not at all well but, during the time I was there, he asked me to read to him from his writings. I found them enthralling, and Stanley asked me to help him with his autobiography. I agreed, but said I would need some expert help. He suggested Wilensky [an art historian]. There was no written record of this agreement and the project had to be left on hold, as Stanley was re-admitted to hospital and died there two months later".

Viscount ASTOR has the following memories:

"I remember first I met Stanley Spencer in 1956 when he came to Cliveden, just across the Thames from Cookham, to draw a pencil sketch of me, following a commission by my father, Bill Astor. I was an extremely bad sitter, a terrible fidget. I was much more interested in following the result from the other side of the canvas than sitting quietly in front of Stanley.

I am sure Stanley was irritated by the behavior of this small seven year old boy, however he was tolerant and forgiving of my enthusiasm for art – so much so that when he came the following summer to paint the portrait of my father I was allowed to sit next to him, my easel next to his easel as we both drew sketches of my father.

Stanley was a wonderful tutor and a kind man. He took time to show me how to square a drawing so it can be transferred to a large canvas.

Only once do I remember him being marginally irritated by my constant demands to borrow his rubber.

I had one of those hard school rubbers which destroyed as much of the paper as it did of the pencil lines, where his rubber was soft and squishy and rubbed out the mistakes without destroying the paper.

From then on I was allowed my first set of oil paints. The portrait of my father now sits in my sister Pauline Case's dining room.

I proudly took that rubber back to school boasting to all my friends how good it was. Despite the fact I won the prep school drawing prize that year, for some reason Stanley's sketches of my father have survived the passage of time – mine sadly have been lost!

Stanley was a frequent visitor for dinner at Cliveden. A car would be sent to Cookham to bring him up the hill to the house. He was always entertaining company whoever he sat next to, whether an important guest like the American Ambassador, the family or us children.

We were always fascinated by the sight of his pyjamas peeping out from beneath his slightly scruffy dinner jacket. He always explained that it made retiring to bed much easier. And he certainly enjoyed the fine wines served at dinner.

My last sight of Stanley was when, with my father, we went to visit him as he lay dying in hospital. Always cheerful, somewhat impish – after all he was very, very small – we left sad but not depressed.

After Stanley's death my father, with friends of Stanley, set up the Spencer Memorial Gallery in Cookham. A gallery to a great artist, who was born, painted and died in the village he loved.

For me he was a painter who mixed family, religion and Cookham into a series of works that develop a humanity that we still see and relate to in his works today. Fifty years after his death Stanley still remains one of the most important British artists of the twentieth century.

I was delighted to become a trustee of the Stanley Spencer Gallery after my father died, as one always remembers those adults who, when one was young, took the trouble to engage one's attention and stretch one's imagination.

William Astor"

Mrs KATE SWANN (née FRANCIS) was born in 1911 on Stanley Spencer's 20th birthday. He paid Mrs Francis a visit to congratulate her. The two families were on friendly terms, as were most of the villagers. Kate still has a Christmas card dated 1908 from Stanley to her older sister: "Cissy and her little brother". Her father Frank was the village baker and one morning in 1932 when he was dozing in a chair (as a baker he started work at 2.00 am), Stanley dropped in and drew him. He promised to return the drawing which had taken him about half an hour to do, but the family forgot all about it. Years later when it came up for sale by auction at Sotheby's Frank's son "Ferdy" went to the sale and bought the drawing of his father for £150.

Kate remembers that a Mrs Parsons used to play the harmonium which was in the little gallery at the east end of the Wesleyan chapel. In the 1920's Kate attended a village concert there. Her first piano lessons were with Stanley's father William Spencer who also instructed her sister on the organ in Holy Trinity Church. Stanley told Kate that he loved "the back view of children".

During his prosperous period when he lived at Lindworth, a large house off the High Street, in Cookham, Kate recalls that a Mrs Johnson looked after him, and did his housework and shopping. He had to have special bottled water for his renal colic. In 1934 the kidney stone was successfully crushed in an operation. Kate was told that Annie Slack a relative of his mother's was the figure in the background of his painting *Sarah Tubb and the Heavenly Visitors*.

In complete contrast **Miss PRUE WALLIS – MYERS** writes that as an art student she learnt more about drawing and the aspirations of art from Stanley Spencer than from anyone else. "He had such a lively, cheerful outgoing nature. He wanted to share his discoveries, some about technique, others on how to observe, select and compare with complete concentration. This was quite masterly and it has inspired me all these years since".

When Prue was a student at Epsom Art School in 1938-1939 Stanley visited the school while the subject of Tradition was being debated. She remembers that "his attitude to the whole idea was unique". He said: "Beethoven may have written his compositions by musical laws of learning and theory ... but sometimes there comes a part of the composition when he defies all laws and does something completely different. He has thrown tradition overboard and used his own instinct instead".

On the subject of architecture, Stanley said: "The poor architect is forced to think of everybody but himself when designing a house. They will have to become paupers to make architecture really good". (This was implying that the wealthy who commissioned buildings had no taste).

Referring to a commission to do a series of posters for the Transport Board, Spencer submitted an illustration that was rejected because it did not instantly "hit you in the eye". The artist wondered how the Board knew that "the public preferred to be hit in the eyes, rather than view an oil painting". He added: "There seems to be a great wall dividing the public from the artist ... but art must rule in the end".

During World War II, Prue had been invited to see the ship-building drawings at Mrs Harter's, a relative who looked after the daughters from time to time. Stanley and Hilda were visiting Shirin and talking about drawing her; Stanley said that it was his job to find out the characteristics of shapes in a person ... sometimes they brought out the person's character. "Just think", he said, "of a father drawing and looking for the first time at his half-grown-up daughter, how he would dwell on all the shapes and points of her head and expression". He wondered why it was so difficult for artists to find models. "You would think people would be pleased to oblige", the artist mused, "but not so". He wondered if Rembrandt or Rubens had a regular array of models always ready to supply any kind of pose. Hilda said she supposed they always had their wives, but he replied they often wouldn't do, just because they were their wives!

Stanley did a good imitation of the strict Mrs Harter: "Children", he said, "it is time you put away those books *at once*". His clever mimicry always raised a laugh, Prue recalls.

"He reminisced about his childhood and the difficult time his mother had getting him and his brothers cleaned up to go to his father's church in the morning and his mother's (Wesleyan chapel) in the evening. He and his brother Gilbert hated the evening attendance at chapel because it was so emotional. They used to try and squeeze their way out before the end … The speaker would get up and say: "Is there any poor unfortunate person here who does not feel he is in the presence of God – come forward!" then while everyone was praying some dark figure would slide past them and scuttle out into the darkness. Stanley said it was bad to work on the emotions of others. It showed that they were empty inside to need such stimulation.

"He then went on to show his drawings for the ship-building series and comment on them. He described the men bending pipes in the shipyard and turning great coils of steel, cutting them into shapes with huge cutting machines weighing tons and looking like the paws of some great monster. Then the pipes were joined together by electricity. As the drawings were unrolled they showed different parts of the ship being made. The designs were so cleverly worked out that the workmen and their materials were intertwined to fill certain shapes and patterns. The men shaping pipes were standing one behind the other, all in view yet getting smaller and smaller in perspective … One man is brushing with a wonderful sweep and rhythm to his body. Stanley said he remembered with delight how this figure just fitted the 'v' shaped space for it. All the work was done manually when the metal had cooled to the right temperature. In the designs men were tucked in and out of the planks. Some at work, others chatting. They all wore coats and hats – Stanley said this was characteristic of the people. He told us how they had to hammer inside a steel tube with a rod that worked with a springing back motion. There were small boys who fetched and carried tools for the men. They had learnt how to move quickly amongst all the materials on the ground. Stanley even explained the different ways they moved – some swaggering, others alert and quick. Then there were men pushing and pulling huge shapes of steel with ropes. The action was terrific, they pulled from their shoulders. Another picture showed men boring holes in red hot plates of steel".

The writer tells how Stanley lodged in the cottage of a Clydeside craftsman, while he was working at Glasgow. The men called him their "mascot", not only on account of his size, but also because of his great interest and enthusiasm for their work.

"If he was unable to sketch the men at work, he would practise the positions they took, and looking in the mirror draw the result. He borrowed a pair of trousers from a boy so that he could study the folds that the man would make while he was working. That was the kind of detail that he pursued".

Stanley amused the art students with his description of a visit to the Admiralty to see Sir Kenneth Clark: "Taking the roll of his pencilled studies of the Clydeside workers out of his pocket, he showed them to Clark in a light-hearted way. He said he felt so grand coming out of the Admiralty with all his work in his pocket. He felt he was floating on a sea of Admirals!" The studies were drawn on a roll of lavatory paper.

———————————

Miss LISL MALKIN recalls: "The first time I met Stanley was in 1941 when I was fourteen years old. When he arrived at Mrs Harter's house in Epsom, Surrey, where I was staying at the time, I went with her to answer the door. There stood Stanley with his little case holding his paints.

"Where is your luggage?" Mrs Harter asked.
"It's right here," he answered.
"I don't mean your paints, Stanley, I mean your clothes".

Stanley then stretched out one leg, pointed down, pulled up his trouser and said, "Here are my pyjamas", and pulling his hand out of his jacket pocket, he triumphantly declared: "And here is my toothbrush".

Mrs Harter's face turned white. I thought she was going to faint. I knew that she was a martinet to conventional behaviour.

I also remember when we were all sitting round the table for afternoon tea and I was being told off for something, I looked up and caught Stanley winking at me with a smile. As soon as Mrs Harter left the room he said: "Don't take everything she says to heart. You are fine".

"That meant a lot to me because I felt like an outsider as the refugee from Vienna, and was desperate to be accepted. I think he also felt somewhat the same way, which created a bond between us, though I was not aware of it at the time. I just felt I had an ally. Shirin and Unity were very nice to me, but did not have the power to speak up for me".

Once, Mrs Harter admonished Stanley with: "I don't know why you can't make a living. Look at your brother Gilbert, he has a wife and child and is supporting his family". Stanley replied: "I have two wives and two children".

"When his first wife, Hilda came to visit, Stanley said he wanted to make a sketch of me for my mother. I did not want to sit still long enough, so Hilda offered to read some of my homework to me while Stanley drew me.

"I watched him paint panels of *Shipbuilders on the Clyde,* for which he had been commissioned. He explained to me the section of the welders he was painting at that time – partly from memory, and partly from bits of paper strewn around, or that he pulled out of his pockets.

"When it was my turn to bring early morning tea to everyone, I noticed many books on the floor and bedside table in Stanley's room. His interest was vast, ranging from *Alice in Wonderland* to Churchill's writings. He may have criticised the government on occasions, but if somebody else said something negative he turned fiercely loyal.

"His friend Daphne came for tea quite often. When he wanted to avoid her, he asked my advice on various buses or trains to get him to London.

"I returned to England from the US in 1952. Shirin and Unity arranged a party for me in Hampstead. I was happy as well as flattered, that Stanley came especially from Wales, where I believe he had been living at the time. He also wrote a couple of letters to me".

———————————

Remembrances of **Mrs ELIZABETH STACEY** and **Mrs RACHEL ANSARI** (née KENNEDY).

My main memory of Stanley Spencer is of listening to him talking during a meal, probably supper with my parents, in particular my father Richard Kennedy plus possibly other guests all paying him rapt attention. This would have been first in a small terraced house in Marlow, which we moved into in May 1947, and later at Woodcote in Maidenhead, the house my younger sister Rachel is still living in.

Stanley had been at the Slade art school at the same time as my father's uncle George Kennedy, the architect, and I suspect when Uncle George heard that we were going to be living in Marlow, a mere four miles from Cookham, he suggested to my father that he call on Stanley. Uncle George may well have known Stanley before meeting up at the Slade, his father had been the painter, Charles Napier Kennedy, and the family had been living, or possibly holidaying in the Cookham area. I remember my mother pointing out a house that had been occupied by my father's grandmother Lucy Kennedy, the widow of Charles Napier Kennedy. My father's widowed mother, Norah Kennedy was living in Cookham Dean in a house built for Richard's father in 1908. I think it was through Stanley that Richard met Jack Ricardo. Jack, a prominent Cookham resident, was a long-term friend and supporter of Stanley, and he and his family became very good friends of ours.

I believe we saw more of Stanley when we were living in Marlow than when we were in Maidenhead. My sister Rachel has a marvellous memory of Jack and Stanley walking over to Marlow when Richard was away and Olive had decided to go to bed early. They woke our mother up by throwing stones at the bedroom window. She invited them in, and Jack and Stanley proceeded to make a supper of scrambled eggs on toast. A good time was had by all.

Rachel's other memory was of being drawn by Stanley after we had moved to Maidenhead in May 1955. Rachel was eight at the time, and to distract her Stanley encouraged her to play the recorder! It was after this that we began to see rather less of Stanley. He had become famous and got taken up by all sorts of posh people who, I think, didn't have his interests at heart. They assumed that he was very well off, which wasn't true; he'd lost his house to Patricia (his second wife) and lived on what Tooth [his agent] paid him each week in return for taking all his work. I believe the sum was about a fiver a week, which even in the 1950s, was not a great deal.

It was our father Richard who saw the most of him. He worked from home and liked to get out of the house in the evening and walk, or ride a bike to Cookham to see Stanley. Richard told us the story of how, during the First World War, Stanley was spotted by a troop of soldiers turning back to pick up a water-bottle. One was ordered to shoot him for desertion, but luckily Stanley was able to talk him out of doing any such thing!

Mrs VERONICA HOOKER a friend of the Kennedy family, remembers Stanley's warm appreciation of the extra work involved when she and her husband arrived unexpectedly at lunchtime.

"There must have been eight or nine of us, and Olive (Mrs Kennedy) coped magnficently with the meal. When she and her daughters disappeared to do the washing-up, Stanley said he thought they were "wonderful", as he was quite familiar with the drudgery of domestic chores.

On another occasion he was asked to define the word "windfall". "Oh, yes", he replied, "that's a rosy apple lying on the grass".

DAVID RICARDO's memories span two generations. In the late 1920s, when his mother was a teenager learning to drive in the country lanes around Newbury, she sometimes called at the Sandham Memorial Chapel, where Stanley was working on his murals. David asked his mother what they discussed. "Not art", she replied, "we talked about music because we both came from musical families. We had long musical discussions".

As a boy, David made regular visits to Cliveden View, Stanley's Cookham home from 1944-1958. On one occasion the artist was changing a canvas section of the painting *Christ Preaching at Cookham Regatta*. The long picture needed to be rolled up to fit the dimensions of his small bedroom/studio, and therefore had to be painted in sections. David asked how he remembered the colours of the section on the wall, to which Stanley replied that he had a photographic memory of all his paintings. This was proved to be true, David noticed, as the old canvas was a perfect match for the rolled up picture.

Another time when David called at the cottage, Stanley was full of enthusiasm about his latest art form. He had taken lessons in lithography from Henry Trivick, a local art teacher, and had been experimenting in colours. "He fumbled in his bath, which always doubled as a storage area", writes David, "and presented me with a copy of his latest print which he had coloured".

In 1933 Spencer had resigned as an associate member of the Royal Academy, because the committee had rejected two of his pictures for the Summer Exhibition. Seventeen years later, when he was awarded the CBE, the RA invited him to return as a full member. Young David, then aged twelve, accompanied Stanley on the train from Cookham, and both of them were "amazed" at the hero's welcome he received. "All", writes David, "from visitors to staff wanted to shake his hand and congratulate him. I think Stanley was a bit surprised with the welcome, and longed to talk to everyone, but the staff wanted to close down for the night!"

Mrs LYNDA WHITWORTH remembers the celebrations in Cookham for the Jublilee of King George V's twenty-five years on the throne. The Council wanted "a permanent, cheap memorial" and in 1936 it was decided to plant a Jubilee Tree.

Lynda watched as Stanley Spencer painted the sapling on a corner of the Moor at the junction of Berries Road and the High Street. She noticed that "it lined up diagonally with the War Memorial", which he had painted when it was unveiled in 1922.

Miss SONIA REDWAY moved to Cookham with her family in 1937. As a child she was told by her mother "that the funny little man who lived in the large, semi-detached house was a marvellous painter".

"He had asked for permission to sit on our garden wall so that he could paint the roses next door. In time we met Hilda and his two daughters. He was very friendly and loved to talk about his work. I was often introduced to his friends. He said he would like to paint me sometime, but we lost touch when he moved to Cookham Rise" (in 1944).

"I modelled for Dorothy Hepworth, who lived with Patricia Preece. The latter later became Lady Spencer after marrying Stanley. One would never forget Stanley once you had met him, and it was a real privilege to have been his friend".

Mrs CORDELIA ASHWANDEN (née TILDEN) writes:

"When my grandparents came to Cookham during the First World War, they became acquainted with the Spencer family because of music. I remember being told how they went to Hedsor church to hear Stanley's father play the organ. He was an excellent organist, and I believe he also played in Cookham church. I do not remember Stanley's mother ever being mentioned.

"Stanley used to bring eggs to my grandmother, and I remember being told that he was only allowed into the kitchen, and even then he had to sit on a newspaper as he was always covered in paint. He was around in the village when I was growing up and we all knew him quite well, but as children we never realised what a genius he was.

"During his Cookham Exhibition in 1958, he asked me what I thought of his paintings. Since I did not like the scenes of people rising from their graves, and the strange shapes he used when depicting people, I had to think quickly and managed to reply that I liked his countryside pictures. To this day I think that was a clever answer as I was only thirteen at the time".

DAVID ASHWANDEN reminisces:

"Although I had seen Stanley around Cookham and my parents often mentioned him, the first time I really came into contact with him was when he started painting my sister Priscilla. He worked in the front room of Moor Cottage, which is opposite the War Memorial, and painted for most of the morning. He would then have lunch prepared by my mother. This was clearly an event for Stanley and we would sit and chat for a long time about many aspects of the world and life. He was always full of enthusiasm for whatever took his interest at the time and invariably had something interesting, or challenging to say. Priscilla was not well and she found the sittings tiring, so Stanley did not resume work in the afternoon.

"As the painting progressed, Stanley became increasingly frustrated by his dissatisfaction with the details of his composition, particularly with Priscilla's mouth.

He must have repainted it seven or eight times before saying that he could do no more – although he was still not completely happy with the result.

"During lunchtime chats and subsequently, I had the opportunity to discuss in more detail some of Stanley's views and experiences in the world. At the time I was a member of the Bank of England team responsible for watching the economy of China. Stanley's accounts of his travels in China revealed much of interest, confirming the immensity of the country and the apparent enthusiasm of its population for the Communist dream. Stanley was excited by much of what he saw but very realistic about what had been shown to him – "it was what they wanted me to see", he said. It seemed to me, even as a cynical youngster, that he wanted to believe what he was told but was too observant to be completely taken in by it.

"After finishing Priscilla's portrait, Stanley's health deteriorated again and he ventured out less from Fernlea where he was wholly engaged in painting *Christ Preaching at Cookham Regatta*. My mother would go in to see him every evening and find him perched on his ladder although the light was often poor. It soon became clear that he was not eating, or looking after himself, so my mother decided to look after him. She gave him a Thermos of hot soup before he retired for the night, after chivvying him down from his eyrie. It was on one such evening that she found him obviously unwell. He never returned to Fernlea.

"Priscilla's portrait arrived from the framers on the day she died (of leukaemia) and is now in the Herbert Art Gallery, Coventry.

JAMES ASHWANDEN has some youthful memories of the artist:

"Stanley had spent several weeks in our house painting a portrait of my sister Priscilla, who was terminally ill. At the age of six, I had managed to interrupt, or get in the way, on plenty of occasions during the course of the sitting. When Stanley was just completing the finishing touches, my mother prevailed upon him to do a pencil sketch of me. This he graciously agreed to do, even though it was at the end of yet another long day for him.

The drawing did not take him long, but he felt it was important to add a bit of colour to the sketch, especially to capture the checkered pattern of a quaintly ridiculous clip-on bow-tie that I was wearing. Clearly oil paints were not going to be suitable, so I volunteered to fetch my wax crayons. On being presented with these stubby child's tools, Stanley looked at them dubiously and muttered: "I don't know how to use these". Surprised that this painter-chappie was at a loss, I proceeded to instruct him in the art of applying crayon to paper, pointing out that the harder you pressed the better the resulting colour. The finished sketch showed how much of my advice Stanley had taken – why, I think he may even have considered using wax crayons to help him finish off *Christ Preaching at Cookham Regatta!*"

In the 1930s, **Mrs ESILDA MEZULIANIK** (née CASTELLANOS) lived with her English mother in Cookham Dean, an outlying agricultural area of Cookham. Elms Furlong was a large house on a hill. Stanley was a frequent visitor, enjoying numerous meals with the mother and daughter, despite the austerities of the time.

Several times Stanley brought Patricia Preece (uninvited, Esilda recalls), by taxi to Elms Furlong. They talked at length, but Esilda found Patricia "vain and scheming". Stanley was clearly infatuated and "he spoilt her, he was obsessed by her clothes and went to her dress fittings, even questioning the choice of buttons".

Stanley clearly romanticised where clothes were concerned. On one occasion he complimented Esilda on a yellow dress she had worn which "made a lovely rustling sound" when she moved. But the wearer remembers that the dress was of chiffon and did not "rustle".

Flowers for parties at Cliveden View invariably came from the Elms Furlong garden. Esilda delivered them on her bicycle. Daphne, who had a long-time relationship with Stanley, acted as hostess. Good manners were not her forté; on one occasion when she was complimented on the "beautiful flowers", she merely smiled. Esilda stood by in disbelief.

In the 1950s Esilda and her mother were invited to several musical parties at Cliveden View. They usually stayed to the end to help clear up. When Francis Davies, a concert pianist, came, Stanley hired a grand piano for him to play in the small front room of the cottage. On one occasion when all the guests had gone, Stanley and Esilda were praising Francis's playing of a certain Chopin Sonata which they both loved. He then played it again and Esilda, who had a good singing voice, accompanied it with a song, Stanley joined in and conducted with gusto.

The lower Cookham road to Maidenhead runs parallel with the railway for a short distance. When driving Stanley to town on one occasion, Esilda commented on the rusting corrugated iron fence dividing the road from the railway. When she described it as "an eyesore", Stanley contradicted her, claiming that it was a thing of beauty with the light glinting on the rotting metal in a most significant way.

———————

Photographer **JOHN NEAL'S** memories of Stanley Spencer are focused from a variety of angles:

"I first met Stanley during the summer of 1956. I thought he was a very small man to possess such a big reputation. He had a healthy crop of short grey hair; wire-rimmed spectacles; a black overcoat liberally smudged with coloured paints; and if eyes can be described as intelligent, he had very intelligent eyes. He spoke quickly with a clipped delivery and radiated enthusiasm about the subject which had brought us together.

"We met at the Fundamental Research Laboratories of Courtaulds Limited, where I was employed as the staff photographer. Stanley was visiting our cathedral of science and was enthralled by this alternative cultural discipline. He saw attractive forms in the small forests of glass tubing and bubbling retorts He was given the "visitors' lecture" on molecular structure, before seeing my photographs of Dr Conmar Robinson's "atomic models".

"Stanley revelled in the curiously shaped, multi-coloured, egg-sized models. He caressed their characteristic curves and declared that he would like to paint them. His choice of such an unusual subject caused some surprise, and it was suggested that I should assist him in his new studio on the premises – which I did.

"I met Stanley again a year later, when plans were being made for a Spencer Exhibition to raise funds for the repair of the church roof. He asked me to "secure some publicity photographs" for the event. I was delighted to do this and it was during those days of preparation that I began to know the artist on a more personal level. I took many photographs which were published worldwide. They not only helped to make the Exhibition a great success, they also enhanced my career prospects.

"Stanley's studio was his bedroom, and it was here that he conceived and completed his enormous tasks. His canvas would be half unrolled like a Jewish scroll, propped up on a pile of books, and he would stand on a chair to reach the extremities of the canvas. He used very small brushes and the area he was painting was lit by an Anglepoise lamp with a crude blue bulb to simulate daylight. The lamp was also on a pile of books – which the artist moved as required. The labour and effort of minutely painting such a vast canvas must have been exhausting.

"He never seemed to be tired. He had a chirpy, chatty personality and always showed an interest in topical events or local characters. Invariably he "knew their parents", or recalled the adventures of his neighbours. His world seemed to be defined by the Pinder Hall, the Moor, the Tarrystone and his Church. For me he was Mr Cookham.

"As he had no telephone at Cliveden View, I called in person to arrange a session for some photographs to be taken for the Exhibition. On the appointed day, Stanley continued working whilst I tried to secure the picture I wanted without intruding. Sometimes he would pause and doodle, or squeeze a tube of paint. He showed a flattering interest in my photography, regarding me as a fellow-artist. He was interested to learn that my ambition was to have my own business, and that my work at Courtaulds was merely a stepping-stone on the way.

"My photographs of Stanley were the result of our mutual efforts. He would often suggest a different angle or detail of one of his paintings. A session might be interrupted by Stanley's wish to rescue a neighbour's cat from a tree, or his telling me of a line of thought which determined his choice of colour for a picture.

"Sometimes he would put his composition board in various places on the canvas to confirm that the detail within the frame was balanced. He often said that I should photograph his work, not him, but I reminded him that it was pictures of the artist, that would publicize the Exhibition.

"Stanley did not own a car, nor did he want one. His mode of transport for all his painting paraphanalia, an umbrella and a stool, was an old perambulator. To me the image of Stanley with his well-filled pram was iconic, and I wanted to record the spectacle for the Exhibition. I visualised him crossing the bridge on Cookham Moor, with the village in the background.

"As soon as we set out from his cottage in Cookham Rise, a squeaky wheel of the pram loudly proclaimed our progress. Villagers hailed him and stopped to talk. A shop window caught his attention and we discussed his grocery requirements. As the bridge on the Moor came into view, I paused wanting a passing cloud to shade the aggressive sun. Finally a stray dog appeared, followed by more inquisitive visitors. Somehow I captured the picture, but when my back was turned, dear Stanley had responded to a lunch invitation and disappeared into a nearby house. Gathering my cameras, I made for home, realising that "experience" in my craft had advanced another stage.

"During the months after the 1958 Exhibition, Stanley asked me to photograph various paintings and sketches for him. He always insisted that they were "business" requests. I would submit a modest invoice and eventually Stanley would obtain a lift from a neighbour, call at my Maidenhead home and pay the bill. Always, when he offered his cheque, he would say: "Most people don't cash my cheques, they keep them as a memento". As I was newly-married, my priorities were slightly different.

"He visited me at home many times and I have the impression that a friend or neighbour drove him to Maidenhead. He usually stayed for about half an hour, when I suspect the same person returned for him. He told me that he could remember cycling to Maidenhead as a younger man.

"On his first visit I placed a big notice for my wife to see: "Stanley Spencer sat here"! A long admirer of his work, she kept it in place for some time. On his next visit (with a small cheque), I told him how flattered we had been to receive such a distinguished visitor. He quickly deflected our attention to a postcard on the mantelpiece.

"Stanley was a great help in building the foundations of my own business. He recommended me to many of his patrons and clients, who wanted their Spencer works photographed.

"One Sunday afternoon, Mr Justice Roskill (later Lord Justice Roskill) called with his children. He wanted some pencil sketches of them to be photographed. While this was being done, my wife supplied the children with lemonade. The afternoon became a very pleasant social occasion and it would have been totally complete if only Stanley had been there. He was so fond of children and always found time to talk with them.

"Stanley was knighted shortly before his death. He was thrilled, but slightly nervous in anticipation of the ceremony. I had the privilege of knowing and speaking and learning from Stanley at a personal level, and I feel richer for that experience. My career proceeded and I successfully photographed many of the world's celebrities, including foreign royalty and our own two Queens of England".

The following piece is a memory - or quotation - of Stanley's visit to Aldenham School when **ANTHONY WOOD** was a pupil there. An Old Boy, Jack Martineau had presented the school with two pictures for its chapel: *The Crucifixion* and *In Church*. In 1958 when Stanley was a sick man, he was invited to give a Talk about the pictures. Anthony's almost verbatim notes illustrate the deterioration in Stanley's public speaking ability. In lectures and broadcasts prior to his illness, his spontaneous speeches had always been well constructed and clear. At Aldenham the random insights and explanations of his picture *In Church* show his distress.

"Now let's go through it reading from left to right ... This little boy here is me. I always try and put me in if I can. I'm looking at the hymn-board, because I never could remember the number ... my brother could, that's him here, next to me ... I always used to look at this big brass candelabra-gaslight kind of thing. I love its glow... This is the choir, I thought of them as a kind of border – a white edge to the thing ... I love the way they sway ... dipping and tip ... a lovely kind of flow

... they seem to totter. I got the idea from some mountains in Macedonia. They looked like some great Christmas pudding with snow on top. These little white things are hymn-books ... they always seemed to flutter. Who is this? Oh, she was always there ... my mother.

"This side is different from the other - lighter, this yellow cloak, and the children. They make it freer. I hate formality and convention. I like to be free, and children seem to me to convey that freedom ... The kneelers always fascinated me – soft, so bulgy and full of shape ... lovely! And these pipes, all decorated with shapes and ornamentation – you don't see them now ... the Vicar said they had to come down, so they are gone, but I did love them. I suppose even Cookham must change ...

"You know Mr Martineau always drives too fast. I have to keep stopping him, so I can see a group of trees, or boys, still I'm getting him trained ...

"Yes, the central pillar does rather divide the thing ... it's a little out of proportion ... Certainly two quite different moods ..."

Mrs JOY BALLANTYNE (née PULLAN) remembers Stanley calling at their house at teatime and asking for a poached egg and a cup of tea, *which must be served together.* He could be quite autocratic at times.

In 1955 when Joy's brother was in Cliveden Hospital at the same time as Stanley, he drew a pencil sketch of the boy. Later, he made a lithograph out of a portrait drawing he had done of Joy's sister, Caroline, (which was sold at Christie's for £600 in 1998). He invited Caroline out for supper several times, on one occasion with Francis Davies, the pianist. They always went to the King's Arms in the High Street because Stanley had a fondness for Mrs Baker, the proprietress. He admired Caroline's appearance and especially her long hair, which he made her promise not to cut short. "The promise was broken several years later", Joy recalls.

Stanley enjoyed talking about his work with Mrs Pullan, making detailed explanations of how perspective worked. The Pullan children would sometimes turn to their neighbour as a relief from family squabbles. Stanley, for his part, found solace in the Pullans' wild garden.

Joy remembers his "scruffy appearance" and the fact that "he always smelt of turps and paint".

Mrs JANE PARNELL (née GREEN) remembers that her parents, who lived at Cookham Dean, met Stanley through their friend, Marjorie Metz. When he was invited to dinner, he wrote the date on the wall of his cottage, and arrived at 5.00pm. He announced that he had his pyjamas on under his suit and treated them to a monologue of long duration. At a later date he gave teenage Jane a lesson in perspective. On another occasion Jane saw him on the tube in London carrying a picture in a large bag. During the 1950s when she was married and living in Wooster Road, Jane and her family were close neighbours of Stanley, who enjoyed dropping in for "a chat".

Mrs CAROLYN LUCAS (née BOXER) met Stanley for the first time in the grocer's shop when she was a teenager. "He engaged me in earnest conversation", she remembers, "about bell-ringing. My relationship with him grew when he became a regular visitor to the house as my father (Alf Boxer) helped to organise the 1958 Exhibition to raise funds for the repair of the Church roof.

"At a loose end during the school holidays, I would regularly visit the redbrick house in Cookham Rise to watch him paint. Taking a break from painting, I sometimes found him playing his old Bechstein piano, purchased with the money taken at his successful show at the Goupil Gallery. He told me that his famous picture *Resurrection, Cookham*, was exhibited there. Bach was his favourite composer, and although his repertoire was limited, he played well. We would then go up to his sparsely furnished bedroom/studio, consisting of a small bed, a side table, a chair on which was a glass of milk and the remains of a cheese sandwich, two paraffin stoves and a large ornate mantle mirror. He was small in stature and seemed to eat very little at home, which is why I suppose, he often appeared around mealtimes at people's homes for a square meal. One friend said he would arrive unexpectedly "Like a fairy".

"On the end wall in his rather dim bedroom/studio his unfinished painting, *Christ Preaching at Cookham Regatta* was supported, rolled at each end and slowly unwound as he worked along it. I sat on the edge of his bed watching him painstakingly paint blades of grass, or the checks on the boatman's jacket. Dozens of very fine brushes and a multitude of tubes and palettes were scattered about, and on the floor were the working drawings. He asked if I would like to have them, but after he died the painting was unfinished and no one knew of his offer to me. He also suggested to my parents that he paint my portrait, but as one never knew whether he would charge two hundred guineas, or nothing, regrettably, it never happened.

"He painted and talked, I listened. His conversation - about his family, the village, or the painting - was punctuated by sudden memories of childhood, what old mister so-and-so said when he caught Stanley and his brother Gilbert, climbing over a garden fence, or how he and Gilbert read under the dining-room table as children, and about painters he especially admired. Later, when he was seriously ill at Fernlea, his birthplace, I would share Stanley's art books and be allowed to take them home. Giotto and Bosch were favourites and Grunewald's paintings of the Crucifixion he admired greatly.

"He would pop into our house sometimes for cocoa and once accompanied my mother to Maidenhead Hospital when my then baby brother scalded himself by pulling over a teapot. On another occasion, at the front door at midnight, I mentioned that I was attending classes at the Art School to brush up my life drawing skills. He was adamant that drawing was the basis of everything – "It is the bones of the thing". Later he was heard to say: "The brushwork is merely knitting".

"The 1958 Exhibition was a major event in the village and Stanley was in and out of our house providing catalogue notes for my father, selecting pictures to be displayed and generally buoyed up by the prospect of being the centre of attention. Although my father had hand-made a large sign to be propped up against his old pram asking people to respect the fact that Stanley was painting in the churchyard and not to interrupt him, the artist couldn't help himself, and often initiated the conversation, loving nothing so much as an opportunity to socialise.

"Stanley was thrilled to hear that he was to be knighted by the Queen Mother. He had his paint-spattered suit cleaned, and with a new waistcoat, bought by the Vicar's wife, and carrying his medication in a shopping bag, he confided to me that he had his "pyjama trousers on underneath". The day after the investiture, he told me that the Queen Mother had said: "I have wanted to do this for a very long time". To a friend he said: "It was just as if she had said 'Stanley, I've got some marmalade boiling on the stove and I would be very pleased if you would take a jar home with you just for yourself'".

"My husband's aunt was Stanley's cousin, and she supplied some interesting snippets about him in his early painting years. One story was that the couples emerging from the tombs in *The Resurrection* were not all married, but having illicit affairs! 'It caused a bit of a bother in the village', she said. Another incident took place by the river, when Aunt Audrey, as a small child, was told by her mother not to interrupt Cousin Stanley while he was painting. Later, when he was sketching her in her bonnet, she asked 'Why is the sky blue, Cousin Stanley?' To which he replied: 'The sky is always blue in Cookham'".

Ms FAITH O'REILLY (formerly GIBBON) has the following memories:

"On the day that my parents and I moved to our new home in Cookham Rise – the removal van was outside the house – I saw a dark-coated man walking towards us. I immediately recognised him as the great artist, Stanley Spencer, about whom I had just seen an Arts Council film shown to us students at the West Hartlepool College of Art in 1957. I jumped off the van, where I was unloading my paintings, and asked him: 'Are you Stanley Spencer?' His eyes twinkled as he said: 'Yes, I am!'

"It was love at first sight for me - and I said: 'I'm an artist too!' I was a naïve eighteen-year-old at the time. He continued: 'I live at the top of the road. Come and see me at any time'. Thus I became his protégé and friend.

"Well, I was astonished, and couldn't get over the idea that a famous artist lived in a house you could simply go to, and indeed walk into – he never kept his front door locked. When I visited, he led me upstairs and I was knocked out to see his studio. He said: 'I don't really have a "studio", I work in my bedroom', where I saw a huge canvas on the wall (*Christ Preaching at Cookham Regatta*). It was marvellous, I had never seen anything like it. He explained how he worked with tiny brushes, very high quality oil colour and a thinner of poppy oil.

"My tutors had hardly allowed us to use oil paint before we could draw well enough, but they had taught us to use linseed oil with the paint. 'Poppy oil thins and dries quickly', Stanley said, and that's why he used it for this massive work. I knew from that moment that I had discovered a genius in our road, long before the other people of Cookham realised what a remarkable man they had as a neighbour.

"After that I saw Stanley quite often – almost every day – and took my parents to see him too. They sometimes allowed me to invite him home for tea, or supper, and I think that he and my mother got on quite well, as she was pretty eccentric too. My step-father was working in London during the week, so we enjoyed Stanley's company. He liked women, but had nothing good to say about his estranged wife, Patricia. He even played marbles with my little brother, who was charmed by this sweet-natured man who talked all the time.

"For me, it raised my profile at Art School in Maidenhead. He came to a student exhibition, admiring all the work seen, and even came to a student party or two with me. I think he was obviously very lonely at that time, and enjoyed my evident love and admiration for him. At the time I was shy and unsure of myself but deadly serious in my work and wanting to succeed.

"After a year, Stanley became ill and went to live at Fernlea in Cookham High Street. He allowed me – indeed encouraged me – to use his empty home in the Rise as my studio, which was fantastic. Having finished my National Diploma course, I took a part-time job teaching Art to handicapped, or ill children at the Canadian Red Cross Hospital at Cliveden, and supplemented my meagre income by washing dishes in the village.

"After Stanley's awful death – how I did grieve for him – the King's Hall a former Wesleyan chapel, became my studio for a while. When it was taken over for conversion into a Memorial Gallery for Stanley, I was so pleased because at the same time I was moving on, having gained a student post-graduate place at the Royal Academy Schools in London.

"This meant moving away from beautiful Cookham, but I was thrilled to be allowed another three years of full-time painting in central London. I am eternally grateful to all the people who helped me on the way: Joan George, Reca McGibbon, David Ricardo, Henry Trivick, and of course, the *amazing* Stanley Spencer, who I loved so very much and who had encouraged my first exhibition at the Copper Kettle café in 1958".

———————————

Some memories of **Mrs JOAN GEORGE** (née CHORLTON) :

Strife.

My first meeting with Stanley Spencer was at a small party at my mother's Maidenhead flat towards the end of 1954. The artist had come with a barrister friend, Jack Ricardo, who lived in Cookham. Stanley did not drive, so Jack, an admirer of his work, shared much of Stanley's social life when transport was needed. They were an odd couple; the artist a talkative, intuitive extrovert, the lawyer, logical, detached. At the time I was married with a six year old daughter and trying my hand at free-lance journalism. I immediately recognised the artist as a "natural" for an article. Not only was he well-known and slightly eccentric – practical if unworthy reasons for a choice of subject – but there seemed to be an empathy between us which had its roots somewhere in his benevolent view of humanity, his impatience with hypocrisy, a wry sense of humour and that famous Spencer love of "cosiness". These were unusual characteristics to surface at a party, but to me they were inspiring.

For some days afterwards I went around thinking, "I could write about that man, I must write about that man!" I arranged to interview him at his cottage in Cookham Rise, a residential extension of the village developed after the opening of the railway station in the nineteenth century. Although I knew nothing about his work or background, I told myself that intuition was all-important, and I should focus on the personality and vision of Spencer the man.

At the appointed time I knocked on the door of "Cliveden View". Spencer ushered me in, preceding me up the steep little staircase to his studio/bedroom. I soon realised my mistake; Spencer the artist and Spencer the man were indivisible. The large, unfinished canvas on the wall dominated the artist. The small room was full of the tools of his calling – a trestle table, an easel, paints, palettes, brushes, pencils. The furniture was minimal: a small bed in a corner, an imposing Victorian mirror over the mantelpiece and there were two plain chairs.

The interview opened with gentle questioning about my qualifications. What had I read about him? Nothing. Oh, dear, various people had written books about him and they were in the local library. Had I seen his pictures at the Tate Gallery, or anywhere else? No. Then how did I hope to write about him? Deflated and defensive, I tried to explain that it was Spencer, the man, I wanted to write about – the psychology of the artist, his make-up, views, opinions – I wanted to know what made him tick …

Without more ado I was dispatched to the Tate and told to learn something about my subject's work. There was also an impressive little lecture on humility, which I cannot recall in detail, but it seemed entirely appropriate at the time. This was Lesson number one in my Spencer education.

Stanley was acutely sensitive about words, particularly where he, or his work, was concerned. Sometimes it was as if he caught them in mid-air and scrutinised them before passing judgment on their meaning. Anyone who knew him well would remember the quick turn of the head, the raised eyebrow, the quizzical look over his spectacles – the professorial Spencer – questioning not only the choice of words but all that lay behind them. He would have made an impressive teacher, the passionate delivery adding a dramatic edge to any subject.

I did not immediately admire his pictures at the Tate, although I respected the artist's sincerity. I returned to his home knowing that I could not lie, yet determined to be cautious and tactful.

"Well, and what did you think of my pictures?" There were distant volcanic rumblings behind the direct question.

"I found them very interesting," I replied carefully, adding," I particularly admired the precision of your painting of the bricks in *Christ Carrying the Cross.*

The volcano erupted: "You wouldn't have noticed the bloody bricks", he shouted, banging his small, white fist down on the table, "if you had loved my picture!"

So ended the second Lesson. I was a hard case with much to learn. Clearly nothing I wrote would be acceptable to him unless I genuinely loved his work. To understand Spencer, the man, and gain his confidence and trust, I had to learn to see things his way. The intuitive feeling of kinship between us was an aid in that direction. Of course, I should have done my homework - studied his paintings and read what the experts had written – but if I had interviewed him with preconceived ideas and second hand opinions, would that have helped? I learnt much more from Spencer the furious educator than I would have done from contemporary art historians and critics. With each stormy meeting – even the rows had a family feel about them – the lesson was being rammed home: every word I was to write about the artist or his work was of prime importance. To trivialise either, or to be inaccurate, was an offence against human nature, and therefore against God, since the two seemed to be inextricably linked.

I learnt too that to paint beautiful people was no challenge for Spencer. The drive to endow humdrum normality with a God-given light of love was his mission. The ugly people in his paintings represented ordinary folk - the neglected ones, the oddities, the unloved – ugly, perhaps, for the very reason that they had been neglected or unloved. If Lesson one had been on Humility, Lesson two, on Loving his Work, Lesson three was surely Have Compassion for your Fellow Human Beings.

However, I did not always toe the Spencer line. On one occasion I asked him what he thought of Picasso, who I had always regarded as a painters' painter. "Picasso," Stanley spat the name out with venomous passion. "I can draw better than Picasso! Come and look at these". Whereupon, he showed me a folio of drawings for his series *Christ Preaching at Cookham Regatta*.

It was at times like this that I realised there were contradictions – albeit endearing ones – in Stanley's make-up. I believe that his battles with me, during the eight or nine interviews which took place in 1955, could have been reflections of his own inner conflicts. I am certain that he longed to be, not only a celebrated artist, but a great philosopher and visionary, at the same time, giving expression to the everyday activities of ordinary people. Stanley wanted disciples not rivals. I suppose that Picasso posed a threat, and until I could share his vision and get on to his wave-length, maybe in a minor way, I did too.

Students posed no threat, and on one occasion a lad arrived at the cottage when I was there. He had hitch-hiked from Birmingham to show some of his work to the Master. Stanley invited him in with great cordiality, asked his name and agreed to look at his work. I remember thinking that it was mediocre, but Stanley found something good to say about each canvas. Finally he offered constructive criticism in the most tactful manner, before showing the boy some of his own work, explaining various points to him. The student went away clearly delighted with the visit.

So I became a willing, if rebellious, disciple. I showed him drafts of my article as it developed, cutting anything which he regarded as inaccurate or inappropriate. By October, after countless rewrites, it was in the hands of a London agent. Publication was planned to coincide with the opening of Spencer's massive Retrospective Exhibition at the Tate Gallery in November 1955.

It had not been easy to find a market for such an article. I was totally unknown as a writer and had no experience or qualifications as an art critic. Singleness of purpose spurred me on, and at the agent's request I agreed to give the piece a Yorkshire "slant", because the *Yorkshire Post* was prepared to accept it as a contribution to their "Personal Studies" series. This final hurdle was easily jumped with Stanley's co-operation. He told me of his 1947 Exhibition at Temple Newsam, Leeds and his earlier friendship with the Yorkshire artist, Jacob Kramer. Illustrated with one of his early self portraits, the article was published on November 7th 1955. (See Appendix "A"). Later, I received the following letter from Stanley: (See opposite page).

Friendship.

As soon as my article was published, it was as if a barrier had been removed and we could become friends. Until then there had been a certain formality in the relationship: Mr Spencer, Mrs George, and so on. My small daughter, Clare, who sometimes accompanied me to interviews with the artist, once said: "Oh, no! We're not going to see that little man you always have rows with, are we?" That was now past, and there was some basis for friendship. Stanley was fond of my mother, and once said to Clare, "I wish I could draw like you," when he saw her sketching with the unselfconscious ease of a seven year old. I think *my* strongest bond with Stanley was a sense of humour. We were both passable mimics.

We met infrequently during the next two years, though when our paths did cross, all the old buoyancy and fun returned. The banter sometimes

Cliveden View Cookham Rise Berks
Nov 25th 1955.

Dear Mrs Joan George.

I thought your article in
the Yorkshire Post in ~~many~~ many
ways ~~xx~~ was the best that appeared
on me. I must get on with my
work & stop wallowing in the ~~xxx~~.
did you see me with Richard Dimble-
by? just 8 minutes that was all, if
it was as long as that. The B.B.C
has asked me to do another & longer
television but I don't know yet
wether they can manage it.

I don't know if I told you that
at the huge Arts Council party
I was presented to the Queen Mother.
It made up for the fact that in
this very room where we were was
where my drawing show was being
held but had to be temporaly dismantled
for this Arts Council party.

Yours sincerely
Stanley Spencer.

developed into personal reminiscence for Stanley. I used to think that his constant reference to biblical subjects was less an indication of religious zeal, than a prop for the nostalgia of his childhood. He seemed to need to keep these distillations fresh for his spiritual comfort and reassurance.

His gift for teaching found expression in the yawning gaps in my artistic and musical education. In a way his method reflected the current trend of encouraging students to find out for themselves. He would speak with such rapturous enthusiasm about Bach, Beethoven and the piano music of Schumann that I could not get to a concert hall quickly enough to hear these composers with a "new ear". It was the same with art.

In the past I had, through parental influence, tended to dismiss Victorian artists as "sentimental", but Stanley insisted that I should take a closer look, especially at Frederick Walker, whose work he admired unreservedly. I am eternally grateful for these paternalistic nudges; they added a dimension to my life which could have been overlooked, or at best delayed, if we had never met.

In 1957 my mother commissioned him to do a portrait drawing of Clare. He would come to our house in Maidenhead, have a rest in a large armchair, and then set to work. Sitting very close to the child, he would draw with concentrated precision and a well-sharpened pencil for about two hours. My mother and I took it in turns to read aloud for the benefit of the artist and the sitter. Stanley said that he found *Heidi* very soothing! We would then have tea and a talk before I took him back to Cookham in the car. Dissatisfied with his first two drawings he did three, all of which are still in the family, with the added bonus of a sketch of the cat.

It may sound trite, but Stanley had a way with children and old people. If he had never touched a paint-brush in his life, his genius – as I saw it – lay in his perception, and understanding of people. There were exceptions: he once admitted that he was distrustful, and a little frightened of intellectuals. Sensing his meaning, I said: "Sometimes they can't see the wood for the trees". When the right chord was struck, his reaction was immediate. His face animated into a youthful grin, he would say: "Yes, that's it", and follow the train of thought along his personal line, extending and enlarging upon the theme as he went.

I visited his Cookham Exhibition in 1958 with a blind friend. Before she lost her sight, Yvonne, a highly intelligent, sensitive person, had read widely and painted as a hobby. She could remember some of Stanley's paintings, which she had admired. We had planned to walk around the Church and Vicarage where the pictures were shown and I would describe each one to her, but Stanley caught sight of us, and we had the unique experience of having every work lovingly described by the artist. Soon a group of people, formed around us, and as we progressed the following grew. Several times Stanley took Yvonne's hand and gently drew it over the painted surface of the canvas, saying, "Lovely and smooth, isn't it?" Yvonne relished that day in Cookham.

Then a strange thing happened over a cup of tea in the marquee afterwards. Stanley whispered in my ear, "I never know what to say when people ask if I believe in God". I was stunned. This statement from Britain's leading religious artist seemed incredible. The village bustle in the tent made further conversation difficult, so the subject was dropped. After my early struggles to keep the peace, I had maintained a cautious silence on the subject of my own religious beliefs – or lack of them. Perhaps in his intuitive way Stanley had realised this, and the jocular whispered confidence implied a shared scepticism. A week or two later, when I was driving him home from Maidenhead, word for unbelievable word the statement was repeated. Memory plays some cruel tricks, as the ensuing conversation is completely forgotten. There were times when one became punch-drunk with Stanley's volubility. Although the opening subject had seemed so clear and distinct, his very personal vision could easily obscure an explanation for the listener. I became an eavesdropper, straining to understand the torrent of words. It was tiring work.

In June 1958 Stanley was sixty-seven years old. It was hard to believe when he seemed so young in spirit and so overwhelmingly frank about his unfortunate sex-life. The reason he had no telephone, he explained, was because if he had one "Daphne would be after me all the time". He was totally uninhibited in confiding similar intimate relationships to all his friends.

Yet in this penultimate year of his life he seemed to be regaining something of the joy and innocence of his childhood. He loved the adulation which surged over him in the wake of public recognition of his work, and honours - he was knighted in 1959. Sir Stanley had freed himself from the emotional problems and entanglements which had dogged him for most of his adult life. Wistfully he told me: "I could do with another two hundred years of life to catch up with all the work I want to do".

The Last Year.

I had sent Stanley a letter and a card of one of Blake's pictures, for Christmas 1958. Part of my "education" had been a vigorous directive to study Blake's works – artistic and literary. His acknowledgement of my greetings ended on a facetious note:

"Every time I go to Church someone hastens up the church path as I leave and nabs me to do a drawing of one of their children. Thirty pounds per one attendance at church".

I think he forgot the exclamation mark at the end, but can well imagine the grin that would have accompanied the statement. I knew Stanley well enough to realise that the humour would have been swiftly brushed aside as he muttered under his breath, "Damn' nuisance really, when I need time to get on with my Regatta paintings".

A month later, he was in the Canadian Red Cross Hospital at Cliveden. When I visited him he gave a harrowing description of how he had been taken ill suddenly in the night. Living alone and with no telephone, he had shouted for help but no one heard him. He told me that he had felt as if he was blown up with wind and about to explode. Although he was anxious about having an operation, I did not think at the time, that he suspected his illness was cancer.

As soon as he began to feel better, he started drawing (the nurses), and answering the letters of well-wishers. Among them was the following to Claude Brighten, a Cookham resident:

"I possess the large volume on Frederick Walker. I possess the little book on him. I possess the "Cornhill" engravings. I subscribed to his name being re-cut on his grave-stone many years ago, in Hayward Brown's days. I love Frederick Walker dearly and his wit. "The servant who broke his flute and said she didn't". I have always thought and said that he is one of England's greatest artists. Fancy asking me if I know the plaque of F. W. in Cookham [church]. Gilbert and I have both loved and revered F. W. and I cannot understand the Vicar saying no one seems to know about him as I have spoken to the Vicar often. So please attend and say "Stanley and Gilbert Spencer certainly know of this great and delightful man – a true artist".

During his stay in hospital, two patrons, Lord Astor and Mr Jack Martineau, decided that life should be made easier for Stanley in the future. His birthplace in the High Street – built by his grandfather, a master-builder – was for sale. They formed a Trust, and the house was acquired for him. Stanley was quick to point out to me that he had been able to contribute several hundred pounds towards the purchase. There was a telephone at Fernlea; and an unofficial rota of village ladies arranged to "keep an eye on him" and do specific tasks.

He was not alone for long. Francis Davies, a friend and concert pianist, was looking for a home for himself and his grand piano. Stanley gladly rose to the occasion, agreeing to share the house, and pleased with the idea of companionship and music. He had often mentioned Francis to me, and I had assumed that they were contemporaries. Calling at Fernlea one day, I was surprised to meet an athletic-looking young man with a robust, casual air about him. Stanley, still frail and with a chronic sore throat, croaked: "It's marvellous, we have Bach in the mornings and Rachmaninov in the afternoons. It helps tremendously with my work".

Francis needed little persuasion to perform, and even less to give a piece the "full works". That afternoon he played de Falla's *Miller's Dance*. It must have been heard half way down the High Street, for it nearly blasted us through the ceiling of Fernlea's small front room. Stanley explained: "Francis likes the romantics and plays them with fire. People are frightened of fire nowadays, but I like it".

It was at this time that Stanley offered to "have a shot" at a portrait drawing of me. I was a restless sitter and he tired quickly, so he put it on one side, saying he would "have another go" when he was feeling stronger. Of course, that time never came, but I cherish the attempt he made, which is mounted, framed and hung in a place of honour at my home.

His illness returned, and one day when I called he was in the back bedroom at Fernlea, looking like a puckish skeleton propped up by pillows. I was shocked. He held a brown paper-backed book in his skinny white hands, and croaked: "It's no good, they're all inaccurate. I've found three mistakes here, in the first two pages of Eric Newton's book on me". He was anxious about his place in posterity and spoke of sorting out his papers with his daughter, Shirin. At the time I had no idea of the extent of Stanley's "writings". Victor Gollancz, who seemed to be an old friend, had shown an interest in publishing his autobiography.

Francis and his piano meantime had gone, a more attractive offer of accommodation appearing on the horizon. People came and went; there seemed to be too many hours when Stanley was quite alone with his tortured body and brooding thoughts.

The return to hospital was inevitable. Following the colostomy operation, cancer had re-appeared. In his last weeks, as his vocal chords had been affected, we talked in whispers. Finally messages were scribbled on bits of paper. His courage was boundless, he never invited pity, and there was a spectral shadow of the old Stanley in his smile. I saw him just two days before he died. His good friends Rachel and Michael Westropp were with him at the end. Rachel told me: "He slipped away peacefully", on December 14th 1959.

There were police in the village directing traffic for the funeral. Crowds converged on the Church from all directions. Some of Stanley's more memorable utterances were ringing in my ears as I joined the throng. I recognised Faith, a local art student, and good friend, whom I had met through Stanley. We entered the Church together. The Rev. Westropp conducted the service with deep feeling, and the organist played Stanley's favourite Bach, its austere joy seemed to say much that was beyond words. Finally the Vicar announced that Lord Astor would give the Address. Huddled behind a stone pillar, I could not see him, I just hoped he would not "go on" for too long.

Then clear as a bell, Astor's perceptive words fell in unexpected refreshment on my troubled mind. Phrases like: the animation of his talk; the penetration, humour and brilliance of all he said; the extraordinary originality of his ideas; his pleasure in the articulate discussion of his pictures; his interest in the relationship between the sexes, and his judgments, which were shrewd and unexpected, but always charitable.

This evocation of Stanley, in intelligible language and mercifully accurate terms, struck exactly the right note. It helped me, and doubtless many others, to cope with the sense of loss. And there was consolation in the thought that an influential person had emerged so soon, who could accurately interpret at least a part of that complex, but entirely benevolent phenomenon – Stanley Spencer. Another disciple, I thought, thank God.

****

Epilogue

Cookham, 2009.

My dear Stanley,

Like you, I see nothing unusual in the desire to write to someone who has departed this life. As you felt a compulsion to share your thoughts and experiences in letters to your beloved Hilda, so I wish to tell you of some of the extraordinary events that have taken place in Cookham and the wider world since your departure.

Immediately after your death, your daughter Shirin and Unity stayed on in Cookham over Christmas and the New Year, before returning to Hampstead.

Shirin tells me that she took a job teaching music at the Girls' Grammar School in East Ham, which she enjoyed, but soon realised how much she wanted to go back to Africa, not to teach music to white children, but to teach general subjects to African children. So she took a course at the Froebel Institute, then spent two terms at the College of the Ascension in Birmingham before leaving for Tanzania as a member of the Universities Mission to Central Africa.

Trevor Huddlestone was the Bishop of the diocese where she was based. Shirin recalls that although she was only there until the summer of 1970, the time she spent in Tanzania was very significant and she will never forget it. (1)

I had not been happy in Maidenhead, and after an incompatible marriage had ended in divorce, I converted my home into two flats, with a view to moving to Cookham. So when I heard that Shirin and Unity did not want to leave Hampstead, I made enquiries about renting Fernlea. Finally, an agreement was reached whereby they would retain one room for their own use, and I could rent the rest, unfurnished. I felt extremely privileged and moved in with Clare in March 1960.

At the time many of us believed there should be some sort of memorial to you in Cookham, and there was I living in your birthplace! I realised that money and publicity would be needed for a commemoration of any sort, so I noted the names of the publishers of your postcards and prints, tracked them down in London, and persuaded them to sell me the stock at the trade price. The publishers were very supportive, and I decided to open the front room at Fernlea twice a week and - with Faith's help and encouragement - sold the postcards, etc. in aid of a Memorial Fund. The house also became a depository for your memorabilia and a rendezvous for your family and friends to discuss how you could be most suitably commemorated in Cookham, "the village in heaven", as you described it.

I wrote to Mr Shiel, your legal Executor, outlining a suggestion that the front room of your birthplace – Fernlea – might become a modest memorial to you. In May 1960, he replied:

"Although I am very enthusiastic about a local Memorial Room to Stanley, I feel that it is premature to make any arrangements, or to form a committee until we know what we can rely on in the way of his personal effects. I am still waiting to hear from the other Executors whether it is intended to have a National Memorial in London, and until this is settled I think the local one should remain temporarily in abeyance".

Two months later Gerard Shiel brought your agent, Dudley Tooth, to meet me at Fernlea. As your Executors they had reached a decision to have a memorial in Cookham – not London – and the room at Fernlea was to be a first step towards a Memorial Gallery of your works in the village. Lord Astor would back the idea if a suitable building could be found.

The subject became a hot topic in the village – and beyond. Shirin and Unity came often, as did Gilbert, your brother-in-law Dick Carline, and many of your friends, to discuss possible future plans.

During the autumn of 1960, Faith made the King's Hall her temporary studio. As you know, it had been neglected for years, because the Church couldn't afford to maintain it. At the end of November Faith had an exhibition of her work at the Copper Kettle café (now a Chinese restaurant). It was an auspicious occasion. Lord and Lady Astor came to the opening party, and Gilbert, the Westropps, the Shiels and many more of the "Memorial in Cookham" pressure group. Afterwards at Faith's invitation, we walked round to her makeshift studio. Secretly a decision had been reached that the King's Hall should be the future Memorial Gallery.

Gerard Shiel, whose old world courtesy and charm you may remember, was the grey eminence behind these events. He had selected names for a steering committee, which initially he chaired. The first meeting took place at the Vicarage on December 20th. I was appointed Hon. Secretary, Mr Donald Radermacher, a former director of the John Lewis Partnership, was Treasurer. Other members included your daughters, Lord and Lady Astor, the Rev. Michael Westropp, Mrs Lois Ashwanden, a queen bee among the Cookham activists, Mr Frank Sherwin, a local artist, and Mr Urban Stephenson, a young businessman. The Stanley Spencer Memorial Trust was formed with Lord Astor, Mr Shiel and Mr Radermacher as trustees.

Lord Astor chaired the next meeting at which my small enterprise at Fernlea was acknowledged, the takings forming the nucleus of the Trust Fund. Michael Westropp agreed that the Church would lease the King's Hall to the trustees at a peppercorn rent of £10 per annum. Lord Astor volunteered to appeal to all the known owners of your pictures for financial donations, gifts or loans of your works. Mr Rix, a local architect, was to be consulted and plans drawn up for the conversion of the King's Hall into an art gallery. All this happened within a year of your departure!

At a meeting in February 1961 I suggested that a series of musical recitals might be given in the Church to raise funds and public awareness of the Gallery project. With your love of music in mind, I thought this would be an appropriate introduction to our village memorial. Francis Davies had agreed to give two piano recitals, and it was decided that we should ask Marie Collier, a Covent Garden opera singer who lived in Cookham, if she would give a song recital.

The first Piano Recital took place on April 7th, when Lord Astor and Eric Newton, outlined our plans for the Memorial Gallery. A week later, Shirin introduced Marie Collier's Song Recital, which was accompanied by Geoffrey Parsons at the piano. Finally Francis gave his second Recital, which included some of your favourite pieces, played with "fire". I remember that your good friend Marjorie Metz, kindly provided refreshments and a waitress for a party at Fernlea after the last Recital. Somehow we managed to cram about fifty people into your birthplace!

At the next meeting I was able to report that twenty-eight paintings had been promised for the opening season; three were gifts, five on semi-permanent loan and the rest on long-term or six months loan.

When the conversion was well under way – the little gallery at the east end of the Hall which had housed the old harmonium, was demolished, windows were bricked up to provide more hanging space and skylights had been introduced - I met Gerard Shiel and Dudley Tooth there to discuss broadly how the pictures would be hung. We knew that the centre-piece would be your great unfinished *Christ Preaching at Cookham Regatta,* a semi-permanent loan from Lord Astor, who explained that "it was too large for a private house".

In July we had our first meeting in the unfinished Gallery. Twelve of us sat around your old kitchen table, which was later adapted as a showcase. By this time my profits from sales at Fernlea amounted to well over £100, which I kept in a special box marked "Sir Stanley Spencer Memorial Fund".

In August 1961, Victor Gollancz published *Stanley Spencer by his Brother Gilbert,* a very personal, warm account of your shared childhood. You would have enjoyed – and doubtless added to - Gilbert's reminiscences.

In October Unity, Shiel, Sherwin, Tooth and I called at the Gallery to see the new floor being laid. Three weeks later, when all was finished, we held a public meeting there. Chairs and forms were borrowed from the village school and local ladies helped with cleaning and other preparations. We wanted interested people to see the converted building before it was officially opened. Lord Astor gave his usual eloquent explanation of our plans and chaired the meeting.

As you know, Cookham can be highly articulate on such occasions, and the Public Meeting was quite lively. While some fears were expressed about the cost of running the Gallery on a permanent basis, others thought it was an inadequate tribute to you, and that your works should be shown in a larger, purpose-built gallery. Donald Radermacher estimated the annual cost of running the Gallery at £500, including the services of a full-time custodian. The meeting ended with the formation of "The Friends of the Stanley Spencer Gallery", one of Alf Boxer's many practical ideas. Your old friend, Dorothy Upson, the romantic novelist, was elected Chairperson..

Meanwhile a catalogue was being prepared by Alf Boxer and Dudley Tooth. A pensioner of good character (dear Mr Berry), was engaged as custodian, and I transferred my stock to the Gallery, handing over £250 to the Trust Fund.

Your old friend, Sir John Rothenstein, then Director of the Tate Gallery, had agreed to open the Stanley Spencer Gallery in April 1962. Prior to the formal opening, the "Friends" had suggested having a Local Artists' Exhibition from February 17th – 26th. This was agreed, and Unity and Bill Astor promised to exhibit their work. The Exhibition was opened by Lady Astor (Bronwen) and duly filmed by the BBC's Town and Around team. You would have known many of the local artists. Out of the fifty-eight exhibits only twelve were sold. However, a profit of £115 was made for the Fund.

The gifts and loans of your pictures arrived at the Gallery in March. I watched Dudley Tooth supervise the hanging, always done most efficiently by his chauffeur. The collection included many of your most cherished works:

Zacharias and Elizabeth, painted when you were twenty-one; *Saint Veronica Unmasking Christ,* and *Christ Overturning the Moneychanger's Table,* both pictures were from Sir Henry Slesser's oratory in Bourne End. The Imperial War Museum lent two of your paintings from the series, *Shipbuilding on the Clyde.* There were some popular landscapes – you called them "pot-boilers" - including *The May Tree, Bridlepath to Cookham* and *The High Street, Cookham.* As a complete contrast there was *Knowing* from your controversial series, *The Beatitudes of Love,* and a portrait of a Blimpish *Major E.O. Kay.* Dominating all and confronting visitors as they entered the Gallery, was your great unfinished work, *Christ Preaching at Cookham Regatta,* which I had last seen half rolled up on the wall of the front bedroom at Fernlea.

In addition to the paintings, studies and drawings, I believe that at the press show on April 4th, it was your memorabilia – palette, brushes, pencils, spectacles, notebooks, the CBE award, and even the old pram – which attracted great interest and curiosity, giving a cosy, almost domestic, dimension to the Gallery which you would have liked. Marjorie Metz surpassed herself in providing a discreet service and superb refreshments, as she did for many private views to come.

The big day was April 7th 1962, when Michael Westropp returned from his new parish at Windermere, with Rachel, to officiate at a brief service to mark the opening of the Gallery. The church was full when Lord Astor introduced Sir John Rothenstein, who, in his Address, described his long association with you and his admiration of your work. People went in relays to the Gallery, which could not comfortably accommodate more than thirty at a time. For those waiting their turn, the organist played some of your favourite Bach pieces.

Eric Newton gave a succinct verdict on our enterprise: "What Spencer needed was a shrine, not a cathedral, and this is exactly what Cookham has provided".

Gilbert Spencer quoted an inscription, remembered from childhood, on the chapel's wall: "How amiable are thy tabernacles O Lord of Hosts". "Nowhere," Gilbert declared, "would its message be more appropriate, than in this Gallery".

Later I received the following letter from Bill Astor: (See opposite page)

I wonder if you recall having a bet with Gilbert that "they (your Executors) will get that man Collis to write my life". (2) In 1962 you would have won the bet. Collis had been allowed access to all of your writings – contained in two packing-cases and a large trunk – on which to base his biography.

The publication landed like a bombshell in the midst of your family and friends. In some passages Collis had quoted your most intimate thoughts and feelings – which today would not be shocking, but in 1962 the media pounced on your explicit revelations of sacred and profane love; and the book white-washed Patricia's reputation at your expense. Everyone was shocked, and the biography became taboo in Cookham, where Patricia was known as a scheming gold-digger who had led you into a marriage which she had no intention of consummating. In his autobiography, Gilbert reminded us that, after your marriage to her "… Patricia kept a tight hold on your purse and

Cliveden,
Maidenhead. Berks,
Tel: Burnham, 9.

Dear Joan –

I must congratulate you on the success of the gallery & the excellent arrangements for the opening. Everyone enjoyed it & the arrangements you made were perfect. Thank you so very much.

Yours
Bill Astor

property, did up Lindworth extravagantly at your expense, sold it over your head, helped herself to your drawings and exploited the sorry pass to which she had brought you". (3)

Once the trauma of the Collis book, and its aftermath, had been absorbed the success of the Stanley Spencer Gallery could be enjoyed. The public flocked there, school parties and groups came, and comments in the visitors' books were full of praise.

After the birth of your grandson, John, Unity felt great sadness that you and Hilda were not there to enjoy his childhood. She continued painting, enjoyed taking part in different dance groups, and travelling, when John was at boarding-school. (4)

In the late 1960s and early '70s a movement came to England from America called Flower Power. It embodied many of your sentiments – anti-war, free love, rejection of conventions and so on. It produced young people calling themselves "hippies". I think you might have approved of them – until they disappeared under the influence of drugs.

You would be interested to know that several of Hilda's paintings were on show in a "Carline Family" Exhibition at the Leicester Galleries in 1971. Nine years later, another Exhibition: "Spencers and Carlines", was mounted at the Morley Gallery before going on tour to Folkestone and York. Hilda and Unity each had ten pictures on show, you had fifteen, Gilbert eleven and the rest were from the Carline family.

In 1976 your admirer, art historian Carolyn Leder, a long-time member of the Gallery Committee and a Trustee, published her appreciation of the series of pencil compositions you made between 1939 and 1949. After your death Bill Astor acquired the four volumes of the series, containing nearly 150 of your drawings, which are now known as the *Astor Collection*. You may remember writing to Hilda at the time:

"As the possibility of a book being made of my work recedes, I wish as far as possible to make one myself … I have my own opinion of my work … and if I were making a book … it would be in writing and drawing". (5)

The series aptly illustrates the point as many of the drawings are accompanied by text in your own handwriting. Some of the studies evolved into well-known paintings, e.g. *Hilda and I at Burghclere, Hilda Welcomed, the Farm Gate, Woolshop* and several preliminary studies for the Glasgow Resurrection series. Carolyn's book is invaluable as it brings this unique private Collection into the public domain. She describes the works as "both an intense personal statement and a unique achievement in the history of English draughtsmanship".

You identify your favourite subjects as being "the Elsie series" (Elsie, your devoted maid-of-all-work), and the studies of yourself and Hilda.

"In doing figurative compositions", you explain, "I always draw what I myself love, what I feel happy with". (6) The *Astor Collection* exemplifies this.

In 1978 I retired as Hon. Sec. of the Gallery. I had been closely involved with the Gallery for eighteen years and other interests were beginning to creep in, so I felt it was time to go, although I remained an enthusiastic supporter of the Gallery and the activities of the "Friends".

Just twenty years after your passing, a book was published which was said "to give a more balanced view of the paradoxical nature of the artist". (7) Titled: *Stanley Spencer, the Man: Correspondence and Reminiscences,* it was edited by John Rothenstein. Despite the attempt to give a balanced view, your friend had to admit that your writings, at times were "wildly distorting … It is possible, even easy", he noted, "by selection for a specific purpose, to represent him as almost anything from a mystic to a sadist". (8)

Gilbert outlived you by 20 years; he died in 1979 aged 87.

The Royal Academy put on a huge retrospective Exhibition of two hundred and eighty of your works in 1980. I wish you could have seen it. Nearly all of your Burghclere paintings were shown, as well as the Cookham Resurrection the Glasgow pictures and many more of your masterpieces. Sir Hugh Casson, President of the RA, wrote the Foreword to the lavishly illustrated catalogue. Richard Carline contributed: "Stanley Spencer: his Personality and Mode of Life", a fair explanation of part of you, and art historian Andrew Causey wrote a long, learned Introduction: "Stanley Spencer: the Art of his Time". Interestingly he refers to your leaning towards Catholicism in a couple of quotes:

"I cannot get rid of the feeling that the Church of Rome is the only Church," you wrote to your sister Florence in 1918. Then again in the

1930s, Causey notes your regret that, "Since the Reformation the loss of Catholicism meant the loss of knowledge, of perception, of vision, of direction."

Finally Causey concludes that Islam provided you with "the attractive theory of polygamy, an idea which strongly appealed to him as a solution to his complicated relationship with Hilda and Patricia Preece." (9) No comment.

Apart from extensive coverage of the Exhibition in the national and local press, the *New York Times* also had a comprehensive review, which included three of your self-portraits. The writer, Hilton Kramer, observed:

"He was an innocent who desperately needed religious allegory and all those loving evocations of village life as a defence against the outrageous fortune of his own experience. When he turned to Realism, it was an involuntary cry of despair." (10)

To coincide with the Exhibition, the BBC resurrected memories of you from friends in a radio programme titled, *Stanley Spencer: Angels or Dirt.* I did not like the title, but contributed my bit in an interview with others .The BBC also re-issued a documentary film featuring you, with quotes from your writings.

It was around this time that Alec Gardner-Medwin and his family moved into Lindworth, your former home. Alec was a keen amateur artist and a great admirer of your work. He was also a good communicator, and served on the Gallery Committee for many years as chairman, later becoming a trustee.

In celebration of the Gallery's twenty years of existence, your old friend John Rothenstein returned to Cookham. He said you would have been "astonished" if you had seen the Gallery, and described the current exhibition as "very fine".

Returning to family news; when Shirin left Tanzania, she returned to Hampstead, taking part-time jobs teaching English to immigrants, and music in schools and to private pupils. She enjoyed accompanying a Spanish Dancing Group, and taking an adult piano class at the Holloway Institute. She rejoined the Labour Party, and with the enthusiastic cooperation of the local Amnesty Group, she organised a sheet music and record stall in Camden Lock Market. Around this time Shirin moved to a house in Hampstead owned by a friend who had worked in Tanzania. (11)

In 1984 Shirin and Unity decided to sell Fernlea. The asking price for the freehold was £80,000. Today it would be valued at around £700,000. The same figure applies to a "gentrified" Cliveden View because of its association with you. As you will realise, the value of property and pictures has soared since 1959.

Carolyn Leder, known for her special interest in your work, contributed to a series on *Great Artists*. She wrote your biographical details which appear under the heading: "A Likeable Eccentric". Another section is titled: "A Modern Visionary". You are quoted as exclaiming, "What-ho, Giotto!" when you learnt that Mary and Louis Behrend had decided to sponsor the building of the Sandham Memorial Chapel at Burghclere for your First World War paintings. Eleven of them were reproduced in this publication. In addition, the centre two pages featured *Resurrection at Cookham*; *Riveters* also had a double page spread, like the Glasgow *Resurrection Reunion*. There was a piece on the Slade and a photograph of your admired teacher, Henry Tonks. I think you would have enjoyed being part of the *Great Artists* series. (12)

In June 1987 BBC TV film crews invaded Cookham seeking evocative sites for a drama/documentary on your life. Shirin and Unity were to advise on the script, and permit some of your writings (now in the Tate archives) to be used. In August Channel 4, an independent TV outlet, caught the Spencer fever and sent not only cameras, but actors to Cookham. The film, *Stanley's Vision*, was to star Ben Kingsley, a well-known, serious actor. He used my garden extension place as a dressing-room and encouraged me to talk about you. He told me that he liked to "meditate" on the character he was to portray before a performance. This was evident when the half-hour film was shown on TV in 1988. My only criticism was that his "visionary" Stanley lacked your animation.

The BBC's longer, more ambitious film, "*Stanley*", was on our screens a month later. Although it was a sincere production, for me it was Hilda, brilliantly portrayed by Juliet Stevenson, who stole the show. I believe that Carolyn Leder was consulted by the script writers. Shirin, now Vice-President of the "Friends," said that she considered the film a very sympathetic portrait of her father.

All this brought more visitors to the Gallery. The Summer Exhibition, *Stanley and Gilbert in Cookham*, included Miss Pinder-Brown's autograph album. I'm sure you will remember how you and Gilbert did miniature water-colour copies of some of your First World War pictures in the tiny album. Gilbert's daughter, your niece Gillian opened the Exhibition.

I think you would have called farmer Tom Copas of Cookham Dean, "a bit sharpish". In 1989 he put in a planning application to build sixty-five houses on the sixteen acres of Poundfield. Over seven hundred people objected because of the site's proximity to so many of your landscapes and the Englefield paintings. Among the protestors was the President of the Royal Academy! We won the case.

Oddly enough twenty-two years earlier, when I was a member of the Parish Council, the subject of a Conservation Area for Cookham was discussed. In 1967 I reminded the Council that "Cookham was Stanley Spencer country. The whole village should be preserved because it depended very much on its landscape and setting … The proposed development on Terry's Lane and the gravel-digging at White Place Farm were the two main threats to the village. These should be stopped under the Civic Amenities Act as Cookham is the heart of Stanley Spencer country". (13) The Council agreed, the developments were warded off, and I had coined the phrase "Stanley Spencer country".

The centenary of your birth, in 1991, was celebrated in a variety of ways. A monumental biography *Stanley Spencer* appeared, to popular acclaim. One art critic praised the author, Kenneth Pople, for "… this fine study of the artist … becomes an exercise in iconography, and Pople has characteristically chosen individual paintings as the true themes for each chapter of Spencer's mundane and artistic progress". (14) A benign interpretation of one of your many selves!

The Barbican Art Gallery celebrated with an exhibition titled: *Stanley Spencer: the Apotheosis of Love,* which explored your notion of a Church-House, and brought together many of the paintings you had selected for the imagined scheme. They included *The Crucifixion,* which you may remember Jack Martineau commissioned for the chapel of his old school – Aldenham. In 1990 the school sold it for £1.3 million!

Our local Gallery celebrated the centenary with an exhibition, *Cookham, a Village in Heaven,* which was opened by the President of the RA. It included many of your well-known works: *The Last Supper, The Nativity, The Betrayal, The Scarecrow* and your teenage work, *The Fairy on the Water-Lily Leaf.*

In June a Talk and Slide show named *The Achievement of Stanley Spencer* was presented by art historian Richard Cork. Later, a very Stanley-orientated Concert celebrated your birth in Cookham church. It included readings from your letters by a well-known actress, Wendy Craig and actor, Anton Lesser, who played the lead in the film *Stanley.*

On your birthday June 30th, the "Friends" organised a visit to Burghclere, where Carolyn Leder gave a lively, knowledgeable Talk on your paintings in the Chapel.

In the same year a video was made showing many of your favourite places in Cookham and featuring local people talking about you. Finally, a service of thanksgiving for your life and work was held in Cookham church and attended by the Bishop of Oxford and Michael, now Canon Westropp.

The centenary was also a time of conflict in Cookham. A new property developer wanted to build on Poundfield, the meadow you had painted in 1937. The long-established Cookham Society put up a sustained – and expensive – objection to the plan, but lost the case. Permission was granted, until the Environment Minister, Michael Heseltine, heard of the decision, and overturned it, saying: "Stanley Spencer's landscape views should be preserved". (15) Thus your paintings had saved Poundfield and helped to preserve the "village in heaven" once again.

The following year there was a minor celebration for the Gallery's thirtieth birthday. The *Maidenhead Advertiser's* star reporter for Cookham, Val Bootle headed an article: "Faith's Vision meant Chapel became Spencer Memorial", which described how your protégé, Faith Gibbon saw the potential use of her temporary studio as a gallery for your pictures. It was to become the only Memorial Gallery in Britain dedicated to an artist in the village where he was born and worked. (16)

Art historian Keith Bell produced a massive complete catalogue of your works in 1992. *The Times* reviewer described it as "unusually handsome, well-illustrated and meticulously researched". (17)

In 1993, as "As a contribution to Art in the 20th Century", the Royal Mail selected your *St Francis and the Birds* for one of its stamps.

Your old friend Barbara Karmel died in 1994, leaving twelve paintings and drawings to the Cookham Gallery. Known as the Karmel Bequest, it included *Sarah Tubb and the Heavenly Visitors*, *Neighbours* and your original drawings for the Chatto and Windus *Almanack*. Barbara's daughter, Lady Lavinia Wallop opened the Gallery for its Summer Exhibition in 1996. (18)

That same year you were again launched into the world of drama. A three hour play by Pam Gems, *Stanley*, starred Anthony Sher in what was considered the best yet interpretation of you. Cookham devotees flocked to the National Theatre to see Sher actually painting on stage, and delivering characteristic lines such as: "Like the saint, the artist performs miracles, with God's help, of course. God's at his elbow telling him what to rub out".

The play then went on to America, where it had a successful run on Broadway. (19) In fact it introduced you and your work to a wider American public, paving the way for a retrospective exhibition, *Stanley Spencer: an English Vision*, shown at the Hirshhorn Museum, Washington, before touring to Mexico City and San Francisco. In a long review, the *Washington Post* summed up the three points of your trinity as "sex, place and God". (20) I wonder if you would agree to that over-simplification?

The *New York Times* found *Hilda Welcomed* one of your "most touching paintings, in which Hilda returns to earth to be greeted by Spencer and their daughters and cushioned in the safety net formed by their arms". (21)

Retaining the title *Stanley Spencer: an English Vision*, the art historian Fiona MacCarthy, wrote of your "originality and ambition in tackling vast themes and [your] ability to make connections between childhood experience and adult vision, modern life and biblical lore." She quotes your musing: "Somehow religion was something to do with me, and I was to do with religion. It came into my vision quite naturally, like the sky and the rain." (22)

Moving on to 1998, Shirin and Unity decided to sell many of your drawings, studies, and a few unfinished paintings because they didn't have room to store or hang them all. Christie's devoted a whole day to their sale, and produced a fully illustrated catalogue, which included your daughters' belief that the drawings "offer an opportunity to assess the central role their conception and execution played in [your] art" (23)

I went to the sale and was amazed how highly-prized your work had become. I think the most spectacular bid was £22,000 for your unfinished painting *Hampstead Heath Litter or the Apotheosis of Hilda.*

Two years later, when a popular BBC programme, *The Antiques Roadshow* came to Cliveden, a lady brought your drawing of Mr Francis the baker, dozing in his armchair at home after work in the bakery. She was "delighted, and a little surprised", to learn that it was valued at around £20,000. (24)

As the new century dawned, the Copas family sent alarm bells ringing in Cookham with another application to build houses on Poundfield. Disaster was finally averted on the grounds of access to the site, and the fact that it was "Stanley Spencer Country".

The Tate Gallery is now known as Tate Britain, because it has an offspring across the Thames: Tate Modern. In 2001 Tate Britain mounted an exhibition of more than 100 of your works from galleries and private owners worldwide. A film was shown highlighting the detail of your Burghclere paintings, and a "virtual reality" film was devised to re-create in computer terms, your notion of a Church-House. (25) I think you would have been fascinated by the technological break-through which could have been useful to you in fulfilling your vast dream.

This show was followed by an exhibition at Kendal, Cumbria titled: *Stanley Spencer: Love, Desire, Faith. The Times* noted that: "People were no longer shocked by the rawness and sexual frankness of pictures such as "the leg of mutton" nude (officially titled *The Artist and his Second Wife*) ... whereas fifteen years earlier Sotheby's considered it too outrageous even to reproduce in the sale catalogue. (26) I thought this might make you smile; these days we are so *broadminded!*

The Tate Britain exhibition increased the number of visitors to the Cookham Gallery to a record 18,000 for the year 2001. Chairman of the Trustees, Dick Hurley, reported that "The Gallery has been awarded a certificate registering it with the Museums, Libraries and Archives Commission …This is a most important achievement". (27)

In 2003 Shirin and Unity decided to sell nearly all of Hilda's paintings in their possession. Shirin explained, "There is a full range of work here from the twenties right through, which reflects her talent. We don't have room for them all to be hung, so we hope they will go to good homes. Stanley was a staunch admirer of her work. So much has been written about our parents' marriage, but people don't realise how much he loved her at a practical and physical level. He took the trouble to care for her during her ailments, especially during the war, and when she died he was there at the end. He always loved her". (28) I can imagine how moved you would have been by Shirin's simple statement. It was so true and so sad.

Some years before, Shirin tells me that she had met a professional singer from New Zealand, with whom she later spent a happy year. After her retirement, Shirin continued to teach piano privately, before she moved with her musician friend Margot, to Wales. They love living in the Vale of Glamorgan, where sheep and cows graze contentedly in nearby fields. Shirin has joined the University of the Third Age (U3A), and made many good friends at the church, and the OXFAM shop; she especially enjoys being a member of Margot's extended family, who live in the locality. (29)

I wonder if you remember doing a sketch of Gilbert in Kitty Bailey's autograph book when you were fifteen? Her sister Dorothy gave you and Gilbert painting lessons at the time. Anyway it has come by various routes into the Stanley Spencer Gallery, and is on show with some of your other treasures. Dick Hurley, chair of the Trustees, described it as "a rare item". (30)

Stuart Conlin, a popular newcomer to Cookham, tells me that following a managerial career in the oil industry, he became involved with the Gallery as a volunteer in 1999. His business expertise proved invaluable in spear-heading a successful application for a Heritage Lottery Fund (HLF) grant to modernise the building. This was something unknown in your lifetime. A National Lottery now funds various good causes, which the government should support but doesn't.

In 2005 the Gallery received a grant from the HLF of nearly £900,000 for refurbishment. (31) Although this sounds like a huge amount to update the chapel of your youth, the plans to extend the area in which your pictures could be shown needed almost a million, so generous donations flowed in to fill the gap.

A year later, the building had to be emptied for the extensive refurbishment. Your works found a temporary home at Reading Museum, where the exhibition was titled: *Stanley Spencer: Painting Paradise.* One critic observed: "The entire collection … can be displayed together because Cookham's gallery is too small, and cannot show to proper advantage its unfinished masterpiece, the five metre long *Christ Preaching at Cookham Regatta* … " (32)

Meanwhile, Stuart Conlin and Dick Hurley were working "in close partnership" directing architects, contractors, electricians and others involved in the modernisation. Stuart recalls that it "required almost daily attention from both of us for nearly two years". Their work included the administration of grants and control of budgets. (33)

While all this was happening, your *Shipbuilding on the Clyde* series was deteriorating at the Imperial War Museum. It was estimated that "£120,000 was needed for restorers to touch up some of the colouring, make improvements to the canvas and re-frame them." (34) Sir Alex Ferguson, the manager of Manchester United football team, and a Glasgow man, said: "My family worked in those yards and Spencer captured the conditions they worked in. I'm so impressed by them [the paintings]. They are definitely worth preserving". (35) I think you would approve of this new type of patron. He has saved the series.

In September 2007 the miracle in Cookham was open to public view. The Victorian-Gothic windows at the Sutton Road end were now revealed. A new staircase – and lift – led to a mezzanine floor! Yes, would you believe, the roof of the old chapel was raised so that additional space could be used. Now more of your drawings can be hung, and shelves provide space for a substantial archive of books and files for the use of students and others. New technology is much in evidence: a screen shows photographs and films of you and your work. There are recorded memories of you from your friends and acquaintances. The computer presentation runs for thirty minutes, and includes earphones.

To conform to modern standards, there is now "disability access" to the Gallery; the old wooden doors have been replaced by thick, opaque glass – frosted like a blind eye. A computer-operated door on the left of the porch opens automatically, and you are immediately confronted by your old friend Reca McGibbon's bust of you on a pedestal. Then another door opens, and there is *Christ Preaching at Cookham Regatta* in its fully-extended glory. A rota of voluntary custodians has to learn how to use a computer for admissions and sales. Part of the Gallery is like a discreet little shop. All this computerisation is the result of your phenomenal success. The pictures are now so valuable that they have to be kept under strict conditions of humidity and security for insurance purposes. So, like it or loathe it, it has to be done! The size of the Gallery still ensures a measure of "cosiness", and the fact that each year it attracts a larger number of visitors is evidence, not only of its success, but also of your longed-for place in posterity especially in that "suburb of heaven" - Cookham.

Unity approves of the new-look Gallery and believes that it will appeal to young people, which is important.

She tells me that from October 2007 – January 2008 the Museum and Art Gallery at Ghent, Belgium mounted an exhibition: *British Vision* which featured 200 years of British art, from 1750-1950. The show was inspired by the Director's admiration of your work. Your grandson, John counted fifteen of your pictures among the finest works of British artists. Unity thought it was one of the "most amazing" exhibitions she had ever seen. (36)

Furthermore, she adds: "Stanley's work is well-known in New Zealand, Australia and the USA, and to some extent in Canada. Europe is still a bit prejudiced about British Art, but even the Pompidou Centre owns two drawings by Stanley! ... I was in New Zealand in 2004 when a lovely touring exhibition of his work was on show ... Last year, Shirin and I and Adrian Glew from Tate Archive, were in conversation together in front of an invited audience, at a small, lovely exhibition of his work in Tate Liverpool. More recently, some cousins and I attended the opening of another great Spencer Exhibition at the York Art Gallery. This sort of thing has been going on over the past years pretty regularly.

"Burghclere now has a wonderful curator, who brings more and more people to the Chapel, including children. People are always deeply touched or moved, by being in the Chapel, and we went there a couple of years ago for a simple service and celebration of its opening eighty years ago. Apparently Daddy and Mummy were not invited to the original service, which seems very odd". (37)

Shirin and Unity believe that you give people "hope" in your paintings; that you are an "optimist" and "humane", although life for you was "difficult at times."

The years 1958 and 1959 were difficult for me too. Before your illness became terminal I always found our meetings – often with Francis - characterised by your spontaneity and wit, inspired me to react in a similar vein. This stimulation replaced my despondency with feelings of uplift - even joy. This is my unforgettable legacy from you, Stanley, for which I am eternally grateful.

With love from your erstwhile rebellious disciple,

Joan.

****

Epilogue. Notes and References.

1. Courtesy of Shirin Spencer
2. Gilbert Spencer, R.A., *Memoirs of a Painter,* Chatto & Windus, 1974, p.184
3. Ibid., p.201
4. Courtesy of Unity Spencer
5. Quoted by Carolyn Leder, *The Astor Collection,* Thomas Gibson, publisher, London, 1976, p.10.
6. Carolyn Leder, *The Astor Collection,* p.13.
7. *Maidenhead Advertiser*
8. John Rothenstein (Ed.) *Stanley Spencer, The Man. Correspondence and Reminiscences,* Paul Elek, London, 1979, pp. 9,11
9. *RA Catalogue,* 1980 Stanley Spencer Retrospective Exhibition
10. *New York Times,* 2.11.80, pp.29,31
11. Courtesy of Shirin Spencer
12. *Spencer, The Great Artist,* series, Marshall Cavendish Ltd. London, 1986
13. *Maidenhead Advertiser,* 22.12.67
14. *The Times Saturday Review,* 26.01.91
15. *Maidenhead Advertiser,* 08.03.91
16. Ibid., 15.05.92
17. *The Times,* 19.11.92
18. *Maidenhead Advertiser,* 17.05.96
19. Ibid., 16.08.96
20. *The Washington Post,* 11.10.97
21. *New York Times,* 17.10.97
22. *The Observer Review,* 19.10.97
23. *Christie's Catalogue,* Stanley Spencer Sale, 05.11.98
24. *Maidenhead Advertiser,* 16.03.01
25. Ibid., 08.02.02
26. *The Times,* 16.10.03
27. *Maidenhead Advertiser,* 23.12.05
28. *The Times,* 16.10.03
29. Courtesy of Shirin Spencer
30. *Maidenhead Advertiser,* 15.10.04
31. Ibid., 23.12.05
32. *Financial Times,* 10.11.06, p.13
33. Courtesy of Mr Stuart Conlin
34. *The Sunday Times,* 19.11.06
35. Ibid.
36. Courtesy of Unity Spencer
37. Ibid.

Acknowledgements.

My thanks are due to Ara Sarafian of the Gomidas Institute, for taking on the publication of my work at a time of global financial recession.

Of course, there would be no anthology without contributors, and I am more than grateful for all those "memories" recalled by Stanley's friends and neighbours. The additional insights of his daughters, Shirin and Unity Spencer, add yet another dimension to the artist's creative genius. I am grateful for their permission to reproduce some cherished family photographs.

My sources have included numerous quotes from the Maidenhead Advertiser which I acknowledge with thanks. Over the years I have always found Val Bootle's reports most valuable and well-written. She was a star of "Cookham Notebook!"

I have greatly appreciated Lesley Aston's unstinting encouragement and advice. My thanks also go to Andrew de Mille for his constructive criticism.

I am grateful to my old friend John Neal, who permitted me to use many of his brilliantly-captured photographs of the artist, and was kind enough to sharpen-up old ones for reproduction in the book.

My thanks go to Ann Danks, who kindly steered me through some of the Gallery's archives, and to Chrissy Rosenthal for her practical advice.

I am particularly grateful to Carolyn Leder for reminding me of her invaluable book on *The Astor Collection*. I was thus saved from a serious omission.

As a former Chairman of the Trustees of the Gallery, Dick Hurley has been helpful in reminding me of past milestones in the Gallery's history, assistance which I gratefully acknowledge.

Finally, a word of thanks to all those friends who have cheered me on the way to the completion of this not-so-easy work.

****

PHOTOGRAPHS AND DRAWINGS

Stanley Spencer with his family, c. 1895-96.
Gil and Stanley are either side of their mother. Annie is standing behind them. The other two to the left of the tree are Will (brilliant pianist) and Florence. Percy (architect) is in the tree. Horace (outstanding ~~engineer~~), wearing a sailor suit, stands in front of his father. Sydney (killed in World War I) is sitting on the toy horse. Harold (musician) is on the far right.

✳ con-jurer.

The King's Hall as a reading room c.1911

The "War Artist" at the Imperial War Museum, with part of the Shipbuilding on the Clyde series

Stimulated by the models of molecular structure, 1956

A neighbour's cat attracts his curiosity and sympathy

Perched on a stool placed on a table, the artist works on a section of Christ Preaching at Cookham Regatta

Professorial Stanley in Cookham churchyard

In a corner of the churchyard: L to R. Viscount Astor, Rev Michael Westropp, art historian RHW Wilenski, Stanley, Mrs Rachel Westropp, daughter, Unity

Outside Cookham church, back row: Mr Jack Martineau, Mr Alf Boxer, Tony Vanderfeldt, his mother, Mrs Vanderfeldt, unknown, Rev Westropp. Middle row: Mrs Barbara Proddow, Mr Eddie Smythe, unknown, Mrs Rachel Westropp, Mr Gerard Shiel, Mrs Daisy Brady, Mrs Cora Eldridge. Front row: Unknown, Miss Brown? Stanley, unknown, the two Westropp children and unknown child.

Hilda in thoughtful mood

A young David Ricardo

Clare George aged nine

Eight year old Rachel Kennedy

Stanley Spencer, painter and visionary[*]

by Joan George

STANLEY SPENCER, whose work is the subject of a large retrospective exhibition at the Tate Gallery, London, refers to his 1947 exhibition at Temple Newsam, Leeds as "the best ever" and "like a reunion with old friends". He remains not only one of Britain's most controversial artists but an intuitive thinker of great originality. He does not paint to please but because he *must* convey to canvas the sometimes curious, but always compassionate, visions of his mind.

Now in this 65th year, this explosive *enfant terrible*, with the fringed thatch of grey hair above eyes that would startle the conscience of a bishop, feels more strongly about his ideals of truth and personal liberty even than he does about art. And this idealism stems from his brilliant, versatile Victorian father.

Stanley was the 10th child of William Spencer, teacher of music, organist, poet, supporter of the Church and natural scholar.

"I think it was that my father read the Bible so beautifully which so inspired me in early days" the artist explains, with his unworldly simplicity. That inspiration has endured, for much of his religious work hanging in the Tate today can be identified with these early impressions.

*Published in the Yorkshire Post

Escaping from his mother's teeming kitchen, the child Stanley roamed the lanes of Cookham-on-Thames, his mind's eye peopling the landscape with scenes fresh from his father's Bible. Characteristically, when painting, he treats the Biblical subject ethereally, and places it in a modern setting of photographic accuracy.

Stanley received much of his education from an elder sister who had a small school in the Berkshire village. When the boy's studies became too advanced for the little school William Spencer, who coached all his sons, continued Stanley's instruction.

"Pa was very interested, but a little puzzled, by me," Stanley Spencer recalls. He says he was the most backward of his father's pupils. "He'd say: 'Funny thing, there are all the fields and the cows and the sunsets, and where is he? Up in the attic. I asked him what he's doing and he says, thinking out an idea!'"

Early wish to paint

No one was surprised when Stanley announced that he wanted to paint. The decision was accepted and a year later the Cookham boy was attending the Slade School of Art daily from home.

Graduation with high honours from the Slade in 1912 was followed by a fruitful period of work. Spencer admits that there is a quality of repose in some of these early pictures which is lacking in his later work.

By the time the painter was 23, at the outbreak of World War One, discerning critics had recognized his outstanding talent for dramatic painting. The unmistakable message of urgency in his picture, "The Visitation," held more than a hint of prophecy of Billy Graham's Christianity in the modern idiom which was to follow 40 years later. Enlisting in the RAMC, the promising young artist served in the ranks for five years, saw many of his ideals smashed and (paradoxically) returned to Cookham "... to rescue the peace I experienced from the war."

He planned to do this in the form of murals for a Memorial Chapel. He wanted to immortalize the British soldier at his chores behind the lines, and to depict the resurrection of all soldiers from a communal battlefield grave. Sir William Rothenstein told the Authors' Club in 1932: "Spencer, without any notes, decorated the Chapel at Burghclere with war memories. Go and see that Chapel. His paintings are the greatest piece of imaginative work that has been seen during my lifetime. You have to go back to the greatest Italians to get the height of imaginative conception which he has reached. People will believe, one day, that Stanley Spencer's painting is the most characteristic of our age. I certainly believe it is. There is no art more English than his."

While small, unmilitaristic, disheveled Stanley Spencer was working on his vast designs for the memorial Chapel at Burghclere in 1920, the late Sir Michael Sadler, then Vice Chancellor of Leeds University, was trying to persuade the authorities to commission six young artists to paint large-scale works for the decoration of Leeds Town Hall. As one of the six selected, Spencer made an enthusiastic visit to Yorkshire as the guest of the Leeds artist, Jacob Kramer, who he recalls "showed me everything and took me everywhere. We became good friends, and I consider him to be a very great artist." (An Epstein bust of Kramer is in the Tate's Sculpture Room.)

Both Kramer and Spencer submitted studies for the Town Hall, but the scheme fell through. One of Spencer's paintings was bought, however, by Sir Michael Sadler and is in the present exhibition, under the title, "Second study for the Leeds Decoration." This picture shows a blind alley with textiles hanging over the balconies of the houses, and the surface wheels of a coal-mine in the distance. Impressed by the brawny cleanliness of Yorkshire housewives, the painter included women in the scene, each scrubbing her portion of pavement "down to the kerb."

Earlier, I referred to Stanley Spencer as a thinker. Each of his serious pictures, as opposed to what he calls "pot-boilers" is not the reflection of something seen but the result of contemplation, memory and feeling, welded and fused into an imaginative 'work of art'.

His famous Resurrection series, different parts of which are in permanent collections at the Tate and other galleries comes into this category. The pictures may be regarded as "true Spencers" because the fusion of reality and fantasy is so compatibly achieved.

Artist-philosopher

Through the liberality of his gifts Spencer could have been a philosopher, a politician or a parson. But as a first-class lecturer and a dynamic, intelligent talker, he is restlessly dissatisfied with painting and preaching, even at their best and tries to express every facet of his ideas by writing detailed descriptions to complement his pictures.

Mr Eric Newton, the art critic, calls him an "illustrator" but the late Walter Richard Sickert, writing in 1934 claimed that " … Mr Stanley Spencer holds the two best cards that fate can deal to a painter. In the present, his pictures sell and sell for fair prices. In the future, his work will rank among the masterpieces of all generations …"

If you talk to him of Yorkshire, he recalls a visit to Halifax. His brother-in-law, the late George Carline, was Curator of Halifax Museum, and at one time lived at Stock Lane House, which was associated with the early days of the Halifax wool textile industry.

Painting two landscapes at Halifax, he was pleasantly surprised to find glorious country only a short distance from the town centre.

'Christ at Cookham Regatta'

In his current series "Christ at Cookham Regatta" the artist working in a cottage bedroom in his native Cookham, draws upon his phenomenal visual memory. The scent is a colourful, Edwardian Thames regatta. The river is alive with punts and people and the banks are swarming with village folk who have come to watch "the fun".

But as a dramatic preacher, the artist has something of importance to say about this variegated slice of Edwardian England. He puts Christ in the midst of the people and with a true artist's perception notes their attitudes of incredulous attentiveness. Some of the pictures in the series are finished and are hanging in the present exhibition; but seen without their companions they are like isolated quotations out of context and the artist regrets that they have to be shown thus.

This exhibition is only Spencer's sixth to date, although he has been painting for 40 years. But, if the hundreds of square feet of his murals were broken up into "fashionably sized" pictures, he could, since 1920 have put on a one man show every three years.

Honours

Five years ago this outstanding artist and simple, lovable man humbly removed his spectacles so that the late King could invest him with the insignia of a CBE and in the same year he was promoted to full membership of the Royal Academy.

Public recognition of the diversity of Stanley Spencer's remarkable gifts, his intense sincerity and potential influence in British art, may be slow, but it is as inevitable as the rising of one of this own resurrected figures.

INDEX

Lightning Source UK Ltd.
Milton Keynes UK
30 October 2009

145638UK00001B/2/P

9 781903 656914